Trouble Don't Last Always

Trouble Don't Last Always

✦

When a child becomes a 4-year old parent

Shane Salter

iUniverse, Inc.
New York Lincoln Shanghai

Trouble Don't Last Always
When a child becomes a 4-year old parent

Copyright © 2005 by Shane Salter

iUniverse books may be ordered through booksellers or by contacting:

iUniverse
2021 Pine Lake Road, Suite 100
Lincoln, NE 68512
www.iuniverse.com
1-800-Authors (1-800-288-4677)

ISBN-13: 978-0-595-34796-4 (pbk)
ISBN-13: 978-0-595-79530-7 (ebk)
ISBN-10: 0-595-34796-7 (pbk)
ISBN-10: 0-595-79530-7 (ebk)

Printed in the United States of America

For my mother, grandmother and great-granddad: May you rest knowing that *Trouble did not last always.*

Contents

Acknowledgements

I am eternally grateful to Gloria, my rock and absolute best friend, thanks for standing by me, in spite of me. Without you, so many of my dreams would not have come true. Tiffany, for allowing me to grow up while raising you, please forgive me. My son David, for teaching me there's no secret worth keeping. Shane Rico, for giving us a new song to sing, hang in there son. Courtney thanks for keeping me honest, but I still think some dads *should* take time-outs. Brittney, for your unwavering love and forgiveness, I adore you. Moye and Nigel, thanks for not putting any more X-men in the toilets.

To Mom Mills, thanks for being there when I needed you most. To Pop Moragne, the original inspiration for this book, no one really knows when a seed will take root, thanks for planting the seed. Many new flowers will blossom because you opened your home to a kid in crisis. Thanks Vanessa, you were my guardian angel and never knew it. To Pop Cameron, the second time around is so much better. To Keith, I will always love you; take it from me, some day we'll all be free. To David, Shanique, Omar, Julian, Jacquese, Adrienne, Debbie, Satin, and Leroy, remember our history, keep up the fight, and do not repeat it.

To Kolmac, Michael, Ron, Lonnie, Charles, Jerry, Reese, Alvis and Joe: thanks for helping me remain true during the Christmas and New Year holidays to my conviction that trouble doesn't last always.

Thanks to Arabella, Terry, Carol, Nina, Stephen, Valli, Nathan, Bill, Michael, Eileen, Jaya, Tiffané Dwayne, and Rose for your support, encouragement and contribution to this project. It's been a long time coming. Sen. Landrieu, you have been an unwavering friend and champion for kids, thanks for over a decade of support. Sen. Clinton, from those early days when you convened us at the White House, you've consistently demonstrated that all children in this country matter. New York children and families now have a first rate advocate.

Thank you Dr. Lewis and Mr. Pointer because you listened to that little boy when he was dying, you saved my life. To Mom and Dad Jamison, thanks for all you did to make me what I am and what I am not. You were always more than just my foster parents; I love you.

To those I counted on but did not show up, I love you anyway.

AUTHOR'S NOTE

In some instances, I intentionally withheld the names of my foster parents and relatives, hoping to accord family members a measure of privacy. All other episodes that appear in this book are real and accurate, based on my experience, research and interviews.

The title of this book, *Trouble Don't Last Always*, was inspired by a small choir in Savannah, Georgia who chose the gospel song "I'm So Glad Trouble Don't Last Always" as a selection after I spoke and issued a "Wake Up" call with the intent to recruit foster and adoptive parents for Georgia children. Although suggested by editors, publishers, conference planners and friends, I have consistently resisted the pressure to make the title grammatically correct. I hope after reading this book, you too will be inspired when reminded:

> *"Weeping may endure for a night,*
> *keep the faith, it will be all*
> *right. Trouble don't last always."*

INTRODUCTION

It was not surprising for me to hear that according to recent estimates, only about one third of teen mothers go on to receive a high school diploma after having a child. Nor was it surprising to hear that among young men who have fathered children, less than half-complete school; and those who do are far less likely to pursue additional education. However, although data also suggest that the sons of teen mothers are 13% more likely to end up in prison while teen daughters are 22% more likely to become teen mothers themselves, I was determined not to be in that 13%. Motivated by hope and dreams for a better tomorrow, I did not want to see my daughter Tiffany among that 22% either. This data puts in context the intergenerational struggle of teen pregnancy, neglect and abandonment that led me to share my journey with you. As we recount this experience together, you will meet a boy born to a teenaged mother whose hopes and dreams for her son were shattered by her drug addiction and lack of family support. It is the story of a little boy's dream of finding what his mother was unable to give him, the opportunity to be a child and to grow within a loving family, with a stable home to come back to. This is the story of that little boy's journey through the child welfare system, a journey equally threatening for a child as the streets of New York, Miami, Chicago, Detroit, and Los Angeles or anywhere in America for that matter. It is the story of how, with all odds against him, he survived and emerged more determined than ever to succeed and give back. It is my story but not mine alone. It is a story of a journey that hundreds of thousands of children are enduring in our country, a story for them, with an ending that we can all help to rewrite. I hope that you find something that will challenge you to think of ways to help at least one out of the nearly 600,000 children still traveling this lonely road that snatches childhoods, breaks spirits and kills dreams. It is estimated that each year nearly 20, 000 young people leave the foster care system at age 18 (the age at which most states relinquish responsibility for these youth) without being adopted or returning to families; unfortunately, I am represented in that statistic. However, I am filled with abundant hope that you will be encouraged to individually or perhaps through your fraternity, sorority, place of worship, or community group, to help one child that is not your own receive the love, guidance, and strength that you once needed to grow into a healthy adult.

This is a journey through trouble and triumph; it is a message of hope, inspiration and encouragement. For my young brothers and sisters, I overcame the struggle to tell you, while it may be hard at times, while you may be hurting right now, remember this: Where you are now isn't where you'll always be. There's a dream with your name on it. Chase it down! In those dark moments when you feel, everyone's walked out on you, stand tall, grit and focus. Giving up is never an option. Every experience teaches, prepares and strengthens you. Don't let the pain and heartache someone else caused you, occupy your space and start paying rent! Don't ever give anyone the power to kill your dreams and break your spirit.

While many who have run this race have struggled and fallen, many with similar challenges have made it to the finish line. The fact is the majority of the world does not care that you have been abandoned, abused or neglected; they just expect you to show up anyway. *Show up in school, show up at work, and keep showing up! Reach out and get the help you can, while you can. Work through it, hold on, be strong and never give up.*

Because…

Trouble will come and trouble will go…but the one thing about trouble is…

Trouble Don't Last Always!

1

ONE MORE BABY CHILD BORN

o o o o o o o o o o o o o o o o o o o o o o o o o o o o o o o o o

his first look at the world is through a broken windowpane
beyond that, an alley leading nowhere his future is still unknown,
for the time being
he's just one more baby child born.
V.Simpson

When I was four years old, I became a parent. Of course, I was too young and too small for the responsibility. My 19-year-old mother, who, summoned by her heroin addiction, walked out of our basement apartment in Harlem, leaving me alone to care for my six-month-old brother KB, thrust it upon me. I managed alone for several days until one afternoon I decided to wander outside wearing a dirty diaper and no shoes. I was the older of the two boys; my mother usually left me in charge when she stepped out. She taught me very early how to prepare bottles and change diapers. They called me "Little Man." Indeed, by default I was "the man" of the house. I knew to keep the door locked and never answer it.

On the last day that I saw my mother, her addiction to heroin and alcohol was raging, and once again, as she usually did, she left me in charge. How was I to know it would be the last time I was ever going to see her? Why didn't she come back? Did she just give up? Did she want us in the first place? For many years, those unanswered questions tormented me; the reasons and answers mattered not. I was much too young to figure it out then. All I could do was hope to see her one more time.

Four years old with a six-month—old baby brother to care for, getting through the days and nights without mom was hard. All I wanted back then was to remain a little boy and a big brother, but the day my mom walked out, I instantly became caretaker and parent. There was no getting around it—I was destined to begin parenthood at age four. Perhaps, without fully understanding it herself, from the beginning, my mother, by giving me so much responsibility, was preparing me for this challenge and the struggle that lay ahead.

I took care of little KB in the best way a toddler could. How we managed alone remains a mystery to me. The day our mother departed, there was not much in the house left to eat. After a few days, there was no food at all, and I knew I had to go find some. This, however, meant I would have to disobey my mother. Every time she left us alone, my mom would tell me, *"Never* open the door, *never* leave the house, and *never* let anybody in." Instinctively, I knew I had to ignore her instructions this time, and headed out the door in search of food.

I can only imagine how sad I must have looked, a dirty, barefoot four-year-old rummaging through garbage cans for something to eat. I do not know how long I had been searching through the trash before the police officer, who had been patrolling the neighborhood on foot, discovered me. When he approached, I never thought to run. I suppose I was not afraid. When he asked me where I lived, I disobeyed my mother again and eagerly led him to our apartment. I never should have let him in. But what was I supposed to do? I tried as long as I could to keep it together while she was away, but I just couldn't any longer, and we really needed help. KB was beginning to cry longer and louder now that we were out of milk. All the food was gone. And, several days later, mom still wasn't back. She told me not let anyone in the house, yet there I was, with this police officer walking and looking through the apartment. If it had been a fairytale, the story would end here, just the way it does on television, with the little boy wearing the police officer's hat, eating an ice cream cone and everybody living happily ever after. But that's not how it went. How was I to know how much trouble I was getting my mother in? I certainly had no way of knowing that this was the beginning of the rest of my life without her.

Once the officer was inside the apartment, it was painfully obvious that we had been left unsupervised for more than a few hours. The apartment was filthy and in disarray and all the food was gone. The police officer had no choice but to call the Bureau of Child Welfare.

When the car with the adults arrived to haul KB and me away from our home, I started crying and screaming at the top of my lungs, "I want Sherry! I want Sherry!"

I fought and screamed and cried with everything I had, to stop them from taking us away, until, finally, I fell asleep in the car. It's ironic, but I have no recollection of being frightened while at home, even during the times my mother wasn't there. However, leaving my family, and all that was familiar, petrified me. My next memory is waking up at a strange and new destination. It felt like I was still dreaming because nothing was familiar. Weird people were staring at me; fat with bright red lipstick and lots of make-up.

The strange new destination, it turns out, was the downtown location where they processed kids into foster care. Years later, I would learn through those records that I baffled the caseworkers by repeatedly asking for my brother Pete. This puzzled the authorities since they hadn't seen signs of another child on the premises.

After my initial in-take interview, I underwent a series of evaluations, which included a medical exam to ensure that I was not a carrier of any communicable diseases. My biggest medical problem was severe tooth decay. Because of my mom's lack of prenatal care, I was born with a calcium deficiency, which led to a mouth full of rotten teeth and bad breath. Dental hygiene problems notwithstanding, KB and I were deemed healthy enough to be placed in an emergency foster home that night.

Thanks to an attentive police officer and New York City's Bureau of Child Welfare, we had a place to sleep, food and stability. Such comforts, one might think, would make me feel safe, but I remember those days well. I didn't feel safe at all. In fact, going to my first foster home was traumatic. I didn't want to be in an unfamiliar place with a bunch of strange people. I wanted to be with my mother in our house. For that reason alone, I didn't feel safe. It wasn't long after moving in with my first foster family that I became more confused and numb, and all feelings of security vanished, never to return. It was then that I became my only friend, and my fight for survival on this troubled journey began.

Just hours, after being snatched away from our mother's house, my brother and I arrived at the home of our first foster mother, Miss Fanny. She lived in a New York brownstone just as we had, but unlike my family, she owned hers and the other occupants in the building were her tenants. As she opened her door and ushered us in, I hesitantly entered. With apprehension, I walked down the long corridor while they placed KB in her arms. The living room was bright and sunny and contained a television that made me happy. Delighted, I immediately ran to it and looked around to see what else was in the room.

Miss Fanny's house was crowded with lots of interesting things that were off limits. I received my orders: "Don't touch this. Definitely don't touch that. Never touch that. And under no circumstances are you ever to touch this," she said as she pointed to each object.

It was overwhelming. The impossible no-touch policy was overwhelming too. I wasn't used to so many things in one place. My mom's place was practically bare. The rules were simple—don't touch, sit down, be quiet—if you were over four years old…I couldn't just sit still. I wanted to touch, examine, and play with things, especially the no-touches. After a few slip ups, I suffered the conse-quences: self-containment in the crib that I shared with KB. Since I was small for my age, the two of us comfortably slept together in our very own escape-proof cell. My most vivid memories of our stay with Miss Fanny are of being in the crib and watching a lot of television. It seemed to be on all the time. Television was fine, but why did we have to watch so much of it?

Under her supervision, I got along fine with Miss Fanny's children, but as soon as she left the house, they stopped being nice to me. It was automatic, as if someone flipped a switch or something. Sometimes they would team up and take turns hitting me for no reason at all.

On other days, my 14-year old, foster sister would have me all to herself. One day she took me into a room, undressed me, and had me lay face up on the floor. She undressed too, and gently laid her body on top of mine. She started moving and bouncing up and down on top of me. I don't know how long it lasted, and I didn't know exactly what she was doing at the time, but I remembered whatever she did to me made me feel confused and upset. I don't remember how many other encounters there were. Since I didn't know what she was doing or why she was doing it, I never told on her. What was there to tell? I remember my feelings and attitude changed after that. Miss Fanny probably never imagined why I started acting so different. It's no wonder I started acting more aggressively.

I passed most of my time at Miss Fanny's in the crib. I hardly ever went outside. Maybe Miss Fanny kept us in the crib all the time to keep me from running around and getting into so much trouble. I always seemed to be in trouble. If I wasn't pulling and tangling the scotch tape, I was emptying the salt and pepper-shakers all over the floor. I was an active little guy, who was curious about everything. I wanted to talk and I liked talking. My mother talked to me all the time and answered my questions. But Miss Fanny didn't believe kids should make noise. The old adage "Kids should been seen and not heard" ranked right up there with the no-touch rule. She kept telling me I talked too much and asked too many questions.

When I wasn't getting into trouble, I was wondering where my mother was, and missing her terribly. I didn't know then, and it would be many years before I understood why my family wasn't able to care for us. It seems odd to me that I understood so much about the circumstances that forced me to grow up quickly, but much of the foster care stuff would continue to baffle me for years. I knew that I didn't like living with strange people. I knew that I wanted to be with my real family. My memories of living at Miss. Fanny's are like being enveloped in fog or a dark cloud. I kept thinking and hoping that it would end that I was going to wake up in my mother's arms again. I didn't feel like I belonged there. I felt different from everybody else around me, and not in a good way. I sensed there was something different about me, but I didn't know what. I had no way of expressing what I was feeling, nor did I realize that children who are separated from their birth parents usually have abandonment and trust issues. No one would talk to me about what I was feeling, so I went on pretending I was okay and acting as if I didn't have questions about my family, particularly my mom.

We stayed with Miss Fanny—and I endured the abuse from my foster brother and sister for about a year, while the Child Welfare Bureau worked unsuccessfully to reunite us with our mother or to find relatives we could live with. Neither my mom's mother nor siblings could care for us; Grandma was also a single mother with five children, all-younger than my 19-year-old mom was. Besides, I later learned, Grandma didn't want us anyway. There was no effort to locate my father or anyone on his side of the family. As for my mother, she continued to struggle with alcohol and drugs. It was a battle she would eventually lose. With her children gone, there wasn't much for her to live for. As her pain grew deeper, there just weren't enough drugs to numb it. Whenever friends or family asked about her sons, and they asked often, she had her story down. "They're in Brooklyn with an aunt," she would tell them.

Far better than to hear herself say, "I chose drugs over my kids, and the state took them."

The day the social worker caught up with her, she was barely able to stand on her feet. She worked hard to pull it together long enough to have a reasonable conversation. The social worker was there on a mission to get Sherry to voluntarily relinquish her parental rights so my brother and I could be adopted. My mother just couldn't let us go. She wouldn't, and for the longest time, each subsequent visit from the social worker ended with the same response, "No."

My mother was infamous for her temper, so with each visit the "no" became more animated and the choice words before and after, a bit harsher. On one of the last visits, an altercation ensued as my mother slapped the social worker for accusing her of being unfit to parent because she was an addict.

A few visits later, Sherry voluntarily relinquished her rights, finally admitting that her children deserve, what she could not give them. While all of this was going on, no one ever asked me what I wanted or even talked to me about it. I never even knew she had been found. Why wouldn't my foster mom or my caseworker talk to me about my family? At age five, I knew enough to care about the decisions affecting my brother and me. I quickly learned to do what was expected of me: To keep all my memories, thoughts and opinions locked inside my head. To not ask questions. And to smile as if everything was okay.

Well, nothing in my life was fine. I could not think of anything else but my mother and whether or not she was okay. I know I was the "Little Man" but living in two worlds was rough.

◆   ◆   ◆

The day I was told we were going to long-term foster care, I remember being extremely afraid, even though I didn't understand what it meant. I remember watching Speed Racer and Gigantor, my favorite cartoons, and telling myself every few minutes "It's going to be okay. Sherry's coming to get us. Yes, Sherry is coming to take us home. She always comes back. We're going to be okay." And when they didn't work, I'd start singing one of my favorite songs to make me feel better, at least for a few minutes. I especially remember being comforted by The Beatles, *Let it Be*: "*When I find myself in times of trouble, mother Mary comes to me, speaking words of wisdom, let it be,* " and Simon and Garfunkel's *Mrs. Robinson*,

"God bless you, Mrs. Robinson, heaven holds a place for those who pray." I don't know why, but at age four, I developed a mysterious attachment to those songs; maybe they were my mother's favorites, too. They continue to bring me a sense of comfort when I hear them.

I could find no comfort the morning they came to Miss Fanny's door to take us to our long-term foster care home. Two very large adults filed in to take KB and me away. They were there to help us, to take us to meet our new foster parents, but I was terrified. I screamed, scratched, bit, and cried hysterically. I held on to the walls, the doors, and anything else I could, to keep them from taking me. I was reminded of that day recently while watching the movie "Losing Isaiah." In one particularly gut-wrenching scene, Little Isaiah is distraught over being transported from one home to the next. I was Little Isaiah that day. Watching that scene took me right back to the day we left Miss Fanny's, and for just one moment, I was five again experiencing the pain and anguish of it all.

Just like Isaiah, I was defenseless. I could do nothing to stop them from taking us away. I screamed and cried hoping they would allow us to stay, not so much because I liked living at Miss Fanny's, but because I didn't want to leave, I didn't want to be taken away again to another strange place, where I'd meet new strange people. I could not fight them off, even though I tried. They eventually managed to put me in the car along side KB, where I promptly fell asleep, no doubt from fatigue.

After a short drive, I was awakened and introduced to a dark, complexioned woman with pearly white teeth. She was wearing a red coat with a matching pillbox hat. Her husband, a tall man with a very light complexion and receding hairline, looked distinguished as he stood beside her with his navy blazer and gray slacks. I could not help noticing he had perfect teeth, too. After the formal introductions, I was told that my brother and I were going to be living with them from now on.

2

I DREAMED

 o o o o o o o o o o o o o o o o o o o o o o o o o o o o o o o o o o o

I had a dream of days gone by when hopes were high
and life worth living, I dreamed love will never die
then I dreamed that God would be forgiving,
then tigers came at night and turned my dreams to shame,
Life will not kill the dreams that I dream.
A. Franklin

Doris Maxine Jamison and Robert Louis Jamison were my new foster parents. They told me that they had a son, named Robert, Jr., whom we would meet later. Everybody called him Robbie, they said, and he was about three years older than I was. I was so excited about getting another brother.

They seemed anxious to have us join their family; in part, it could have been because my foster father grew up in an orphanage. Later on, as our relationship grew, he often spoke about his adventures as an orphan during the Depression. He had promised himself that one day he would give to a child the home he had always wanted as a little boy. As the months turned into years with the Jamison, I was grateful he'd kept that promise. First, I had to adjust to a new set of parents, a new older brother, and a new set of rules.

During their first visit to the Catholic Home Bureau, we spent a few minutes of getting acquainted, before my brother KB and I made our way to the Jamison family car—a very sharp red and white Oldsmobile with wings on the back. As KB and I huddled up next to each other in the back seat, I began to feel overwhelmed by everything. The car seemed so big, and I felt so small. I was leaving Miss Fanny and going to live with people we had only just met. I had no idea what awaited us at the Jamison's house. It was a lot for a five-year old-to process.

As we made our way to our new home in Crown Heights, Brooklyn, I remember Mr. Jamison looking in the rear view mirror and asking me a most interesting question: "What do you want to call me and my wife?"

Without hesitation, I said "Mom and Dad."

It would be the first time I had ever called anybody Mom and Dad, and from that moment on, they would always be for KB and me.

When we arrived at our new home, I cautiously scoped out the environment. It was clear to me that this apartment was nothing like any home I had ever seen. It was clean and orderly. The living room had plush rust-colored carpet with plastic slipcovers over the furniture. I had to ask what the big brown wooden thing against the wall was. I'd never seen a piano before. After Dad told me, he said that Robbie takes piano lessons, and that maybe I might someday too. I had no clue what piano lessons were.

The bedroom KB and I shared with Robbie was light green, brightly lit, and very neat. Everything seemed to have its proper place. I remember thinking, "Boy, oh boy, these people have so many nice things." I wasn't used to all this nice stuff. It was even nicer than Miss Fanny's was. She didn't have a piano. Then I started to feel scared. I could not keep still or get comfortable. I could not stop thinking about the big men. Would they come back to take us away?

We were in a poor state of health when we arrived at the Jamison. Diagnosed with calcium deficiency, a condition exacerbated by the fact that my birth mother hated milk, KB's bones were so fragile that, at nearly two years of age, he was still unable to walk.

Shortly after our arrival, Mom Jamison took me to a dentist, who determined that my rotten teeth would have to be extracted if the permanent teeth were to have a chance to grow in correctly. By the time I turned six, I had nine teeth extracted and hideous silver caps placed on the remaining teeth. I thought the caps made me look ugly. They definitely added to my growing sense of feeling different. In an effort to fit in, I would take a safety pin and try to pry them off when no one was looking. One day, I finally succeeded.

I ran to Mom Jamison screaming, "Mom! Mom! Mom! My cap fell off," hoping she would let me leave it off for good.

She didn't.

She promptly took me to the dentist to have it replaced. Boy, did I hate those caps.

On one of our frequent visits to the pediatrician, Mom Jamison was told that being carried too frequently was as much to blame for my baby brother's fragile bones as the calcium deficiency. People picked KB up constantly because he was such an incredibly handsome little boy. No one seemed to realize being lifted so much was discouraging him from walking.

◆   ◆   ◆

Robbie, KB, and I shared a room. Robbie and KB shared the top and bottom of a high riser bed. I had my own folding ottoman. I wanted to share the high riser though. I didn't want to be separate. Maybe this was the sleeping arrangement because I was a bed wetter. On the other hand, was I separated from them because I didn't seem to enjoy being around other kids? The reality was, I was self-conscious and insecure and desperately wanted to fit in. I don't know.

It didn't help matters that my new foster brother Robbie was brilliant, well behaved, and excelling at school. Much to my dismay, he and KB instantly bonded and became very close. I began to resent both of them.

"Robbie is so smart," everyone would say.

"Isn't KB cute? Just look at those big eyes," others would gush.

People never had much to say about me. My breath always stank because of my rotting teeth and I had those awful silver caps. My behavior was not the best either. Sandwiched between Robbie and KB, I was lost. I didn't fit in and no one seemed to notice me. Eventually, I figured out that people paid attention to me when I was in trouble. Therefore, I gave them trouble—and lots of it.

I started stealing and lying shortly after I arrived at the Jamison. The living room was one of my favorite places to hit. Despite having been told, on numerous occasions, that it was off limits unless an adult was present, I ventured in to take whatever was of real interest to me, especially the money. Dad Jamison used to keep excess change hidden on the top shelf of the bookcase. I remember the rush I would get from taking things that belonged to someone else. The real thrill was in knowing that I usually wasn't caught. And even when I did, the attention I received, however negative, and was better than no attention at all.

In addition to thieving, I found myself making up elaborate "stories" as well; hoping people would be impressed and listen to me. I really wanted to be heard. I wanted to be noticed. I was so mixed up inside and in so much pain, and so confused that I was willing to do whatever it took to get attention, even if it meant lying.

Mom Jamison really seemed to like my stories at first. Eventually, however, she and most everyone else caught on, and no one would believe anything I said. I was branded a liar and a thief, a tag that would follow me throughout school.

◆　　　◆　　　◆

I started first grade just before my sixth birthday, a considerable accomplishment given all the drama in my life. At St. Francis of Assisi on Lincoln Road in Brooklyn, all eyes seemed to focus on me with my metallic teeth. To add to my allure, I started wearing glasses. Even I could not deny that I looked like a little geek. My classmates teased me mercilessly. At recess, it was open season and I often found myself the brunt of many a jokester's pranks.

I didn't like myself at all. I was confused and overwhelmed with all that was happening in my life. Interacting with kids who lived with their real parents and shared the same last names would get to me from time to time. They all seemed so perfect and much happier. They certainly didn't get into the amount of trouble that I did.

I couldn't concentrate on my schoolwork. At test time, I always preferred multiple-choice. That way I wouldn't have to focus on reading the question. I just randomly selected a, b, or c. It wasn't that I was lazy; I just couldn't concentrate long enough to read an entire question. Sometimes my multiple-choice method worked and I got good test scores back; other times, I got a glaring D or F, causing my low self-esteem to plummet even farther.

To escape, I did what many children in distress do: I daydreamed a lot, letting my imagination carry me away without warning. I'd drift away in thoughts about my real family: *What are they doing? What do they look like? Do I look like them? Am I that ugly? Why don't they want me? Where is my mother? I wish I could be good. Maybe then, people will like me; maybe I would fit in.* These thoughts consumed me and kept me from being a good student. Seems I was able to concentrate on everything else but school.

I found the rigidity and complexity of Catholic school difficult. There were just too many rules. Not to be deterred, I tested as many of them possible to see how much I could get away with. In short order, I became the class clown. The nuns definitely needed a sense of humor, and who better to entertain them than attention-craved Shane.

I thrived on rattling their cages. (I wonder if I'm the only one who imagined what it would be like to pull a habit off a nun's head.) Because of my constant misbehavior, I lived in the principal's office. Sometimes my teacher, Sister Collette, would punish me by making me sit in a trashcan with my legs hanging out. Then she'd add insult to injury by letting other students empty the shavings from their pencil sharpeners on me.

If I wasn't lying or clowning, I was stealing. My parents would give me money to buy books, but I spent it instead. When I was short on cash, I stole money from my classmates, taking cash from their book bags when they weren't looking. Money my parents gave me for my student savings account never made it to the bank because I spent that too. The sad truth is I thought I was getting over on everybody.

Throughout the second, third, and fourth grades, my reputation as a liar and thief was solidified. I also became known as the kid who couldn't pay attention. My lack of concentration led school administrators to evaluate me for special education classes. No one realized that my real problem was that I had a severe case of Attention Deficit Disorder (ADD). Educators didn't even know ADD existed back then. Fortunately, I was never placed in the special education program. However, my struggle to focus on schoolwork and to concentrate continued. As much as I tried to calm my mind and still my body, I couldn't. I knew there was something different about me. Why I couldn't act and think like the other children? Why was I always in trouble?

At every parent-teacher conference, I would overhear my teachers tell Mom Jamison that I was "not working up to my full potential." That one statement meant extra punishment for not behaving correctly in school. I spent many recesses, timeouts, and afternoons after school standing in the corner facing a wall either angry or confused, or drifting in a daydream. My disruptive, impulsive, and outright aggressive behavior was never associated with a neurological condition that caused my brain to function differently than most others. Without the proper diagnosis and intervention, my reputation as "the worst kid in the classroom" gradually changed to my being considered one of the worst kids in the school.

By the time I entered the fifth grade, all the teachers knew that whoever got Shane as a student was in for a challenge, and they treated me accordingly. Sister Miriam Anita, the meanest nun of them all, constantly threatened to have me, a consummate bad actor, transferred to public school if I continued to misbehave. Public school was the worst possible punishment that could happen to a kid. The nuns were quick to remind anyone who stepped out of line that *those* public school kids were bad. They were *mean*. And kids got beat up there *al the time*. Public school sounded a lot like Catholic school with me as lead character. Regardless, whenever I heard "the threat," I'd straighten up, but not for long. I have Sister Miriam Anita to thank for my sporadic good behavior. However, even with the threat of expulsion, I would revert to acting out and not just at school.

Had the diagnostic tools and resources been available to me then, my early educational experience would have been vastly different. I would have been taught how to adapt to the way my brain functioned. Instead, it seems the goal of my teachers was to change what couldn't be changed. If they had put as much energy into teaching me ways to overcome my learning difficulties, and how to leverage my strengths, I would have been a more confident child and better student. I would not have grown up thinking I was not good in math or struggled through school living out their low expectations of me. Instead, I would have realized much earlier in life that my brain processes information so rapidly that while people are talking I'm often already onto something else. For instance, in math I would often figure out the problem in my head, and stop focusing on the remainder of the lesson. Called upon, I frequently gave the correct answer, but got in trouble when I could not adequately explain the steps I took to arrive at my calculation. The "process thing" just does not work for me. I'd bypass one or more steps and race through the equation. I figured, why go through all of the trouble if there is a more efficient way, or a quicker solution? Well, as I would eventually learn, quick solutions do not apply to everything in life. I just did not learn it in elementary school.

◆   ◆   ◆

During those initial years with the Jamison, we would sometimes visit Mr. Jamison's sister, who we called Aunt Flip. Unlike her older brother, Aunt Flip had very straight hair and looked like a white woman, two traits she took immense pride in. She would tell me the "whiter" I looked and behaved, the more successful I would be in life. She made me pinch my nose so that it wouldn't be so wide. This way, with my "fair" complexion, she reasoned, I could pass for white. Well, my nose is still wide and my skin hasn't lightened over the years, so I guess I won't be passing for white after all. Sorry to disappoint you, Aunt Flip.

One day, while Aunt Flip was babysitting KB and me at her house, I found some matches and decided to sneak into the downstairs bathroom to play with them. I struck a few of them, tossing them in the toilet bowl to extinguish their tiny flames. Intrigued, I set the toilet paper on fire, which very quickly got out of control. Panicked, I threw the roll into the toilet and a huge cloud of smoke billowed out. I ran upstairs yelling and screaming, with every ounce of conviction I could muster, that my "doo-doo" was on fire, hoping Aunt Flip would actually believe that poop was a highly unstable combustible. (I never said I was a good liar.)

When I went home that evening I got my butt tore up. I knew enough to know that foster parents are not supposed to spank children, but the Jamison treated me as their own. That night Mr. Jamison gave me a beating that I will never forget. He said he was beating me out of love, and that I would remember that day as long as I lived. Well, he was right. I never forgot how with every lash of the belt, Mr. Jamison kept telling me why he was beating me and how much he loved me. From that day forward, I never played with matches again.

My relationship with Dad Jamison was different from KB's and Robbie's. He had a ferocious temper, so I was afraid of him just as everyone else in the house was. However, I really did feel that he loved me. He seemed to take genuine interest in spending time with me, and talking to me about the things I liked. We liked many of the same things, for example, watching "60 Minutes" with Mike Wallace on television. Dad enjoyed teaching as much as I enjoyed learning how to fix things around the house. I enjoyed his company, and behaved differently when he was around, a fact that didn't go unnoticed by Mom Jamison. She would often remind me of this split in my personality, when I was acting out in his absence. I believe he was the only person in the house who really understood me.

In retrospect, I think I was his favorite in spite of the fact that I was a bad kid. He saw my potential and understood my pain. He'd been abandoned at birth, too, and had made his way through life without the love, support and nurturance of his parents. Perhaps he saw a bit of himself in me.

My jealously of Robbie and KB continued to grow throughout elementary school. They were so "perfect." Even when they misbehaved, things just seemed to turn out better for them. KB, the cute one and the youngest, floated on a stream of constant compliments and attention. He was smart too, and I hated that. One day we were running through the house, and knowing he was a few feet behind me, I intentionally slammed a door shut. He crashed into the door hitting it so hard he was knocked unconscious. I was actually scared when I saw my brother stretched out on the floor. His big lips turned blue, and Mom Jamison had to use smelling salts to bring him to. Then she knocked the living daylights out of me. That whipping, I deserved.

As if having a real mother and father weren't enough of a reason to resent Robbie, he also turned out to be a child prodigy. He spoke three different languages and played six musical instruments. Unbelievable! I spent many an evening at Carnegie Hall listening to Robbie's musical recitals. Ultimately, my resentment towards Robbie grew to the point of violence. One day I punched him, without provocation, in the stomach as hard as I could. I knew he was soft and would not fight back so I wasn't surprised when he went crying to Mom.

Her response, "If you won't defend yourself, you deserved it."

That may have been a good lesson in self-defense for Robbie, but not for an angry, jealous brother. From that day forward, I ruled both my older foster brother and my younger brother, but my satisfaction was fleeting. Stuck between the two of them, adorable KB and Robbie, the genius, shameless Shane was in a difficult situation. The older I got, the worse I felt about myself. My self-esteem continued to spiral downhill. It didn't help that I frowned a lot. I avoided smiling because of those silver-capped teeth and because Mom Jamison often said to me that, I smiled like a monkey. Then there were the glasses. Aunt Flip said they made me look like an owl. The other kids thought the glasses had more of a "point-Dexter" mystique and teased me every chance they got. I was in turmoil, unhappy and lonely because I did not fit in. I could not stop wetting the bed, a constant source of embarrassment and shame, no matter how hard I tried. It seemed as if no one liked me or understood me. I just did not belong anywhere. And based on everything I was hearing from my caregivers, I was a monkey-grinning, owl-faced, bed-wetting liar and thief. Not a great self-image for anyone, especially a child desperately in need of his mother's love.

◆   ◆   ◆

As if I wasn't already confused, puberty kicked in and Paulette caught my eye. At age thirteen, she was choc-o-late, with kinky hair, rough, and I liked it. Paulette lived down the street and sometimes we'd play house in the stairwell of the six-story building where I lived. That's where she taught me "the nasty." I had no idea my body could feel and do the things it did on the roof that day. It felt good, but I didn't understand what she had done to me. The excitement of having sex was a little bit scary at first.

Pleasure won out over fear because soon after my first encounter with Paulette, I tried several times to make myself feel and do those things again. How Mom Jamison figured out what I was up to in the privacy of the locked bathroom, I'll never know. But one day, I overheard her asking Robbie what he thought she should do about my self-discovery.

"Leave him alone, its normal," Robbie insisted.

As close as I felt to Dad Jamison, I was uncomfortable asking him about sex, and going to Mom Jamison was definitely out of the question. She was stern and against her better judgment, overlooked my indiscretion. Since mom never broached the subject, I eventually I went to the neighborhood library and found books on human sexuality to help me understand what I was experiencing.

Paulette and I continued our secret rooftop rendezvous, which I never told anyone about. What would they think if they knew I was "doing it" and having all these strange new feelings on top of my behavior problems?

Months later, at a children's Halloween party, I had a different kind of sexual encounter with the host of the party—a white man who lived across the street from us. Midway through the party, he led me to his basement. I remember thinking, where is everyone? How did I wind up left down here alone with this fat greasy-looking white man? Where was Robbie? Then he started touching me all over. I started to run around the chairs scattered about from playing musical chairs. I ran up the steps and the door was locked. He called after me. I do not remember exactly what he said, but it was something along the lines of "big boys don't run" and then he unlocked the door, and I ran home.

Another time, while I was playing in front of my building, the same man offered me potato chips, if I'd let him touch me again. I like chips but did not get in the car that time. Just looking at him made me sick. I later learned he had molested another child in the neighborhood. Even though I never told Mom and Dad Jamison about the incidents, I was fortunate to have an adult in my life that I felt comfortable confiding in; Dr. Lewis, my therapist, listened and reassured me that it was not my fault, that I had done nothing wrong. It wasn't until I became an advocate for children that I learned the alarming statistics related to child molestation: One out of every four girls is molested, and one out of every five boys, before they reach the age of eighteen.

◆　　　◆　　　◆

Like most kids my age, I wanted to have my own pocket money. I was lucky enough to get a paper route. The pay was good, and the tips were great. I'd been on the job for a few weeks, when one day on one of my regular stops, I rang the front doorbell and no one answered. I turned the knob and the door opened. While standing in the doorway, I saw a pair of pants hanging over a chair. I couldn't resist pushing the door all the way open, sneaking inside, and going through the pockets. I left the newspaper (as evidence, of course) and raced out of the apartment. I don't remember how much money I got, but I felt rich. It was like Christmas in July. I went down the street to the store and bought a tape recorder and a bunch of other things.

When I got home and Mom Jamison saw my new purchases, she correctly deduced that I had stolen the money and was convinced I had taken it from her purse. Dad Jamison also thought that I had stolen the money, but from his stash in the living room. What hypocrites, I thought. Here they were chastising me for stealing, and both of them were trying to claim something that did not belong to either of them. It never dawned on me that there might be another thief in our midst. Was I the only Jamison boy with sticky fingers? Of course, Prince KB and Sir Robbie would never stoop so low. I listened in silence as my accusers argued over whose money had been lifted. If they knew where I had really gotten it from, it would have made the situation worse, so I never uttered a word.

Confused, distressed, and plagued by trouble, I concluded that the best solution for my problems was to run away. The next Sunday morning, I took all of my paper route tips and my newly acquired loot, hooked up with my friend Stacey who lived downstairs, and took off. We thought we were set, but the money ran out after our first stop at White Castle for hamburgers and fries. He'd barely licked the grease from his lips, when Stacey punked out and went back home. I didn't want to go back home, but I did. Less than two hours on the road and I was back at the Jamison. No one even knew I was AWOL.

I was so unhappy there. I felt like I couldn't do anything right and that no one liked me. Even Dad Jamison's patience was worn thin. I was eleven years old and had been seeing a therapist for two years. Therapy wasn't helping my image problem either. It only made me feel more different from my brothers and classmates. As my self-esteem fell, my behavior worsened. I told Dr. Lewis, my shrink, about the loneliness I felt. I was beginning to think less often about ever seeing my mother again because I hoped the emptiness I felt would vanish by adopting a new last name.

My arrival at the Jamison's home triggered daydreams of adoption and sharing their surname. For some reason the thought of signing my name as "Shane Jamison" was the most appealing part of having the same last name. Plus, I wanted to belong to someone, to fit in. I wanted the same family name. At least then, people couldn't tell from my name that I was different.

If adoption is permanent, as my therapist told me, then KB and I would be secure for sure. No more sudden moves, no more strange people. In one of my therapy sessions, I wrote a three-page play called, "The Adopted Child." In this play, the Jamison adopted me. In the end, that's all it was, a play.

KB and I lived in the Jamison home for over seven years. Well nurtured, disciplined, and humbled, we were given the best of everything: lots of love, private educations, and the finest clothing. Never did they treat us any differently from their birth son. We even dressed in matching clothing, as if we were triplets. We went to the same private schools, got the same medical care, and shared the same room.

However, the stability they created for me did not change the fact that I was different, an outsider. I always knew I was different. I felt it. I didn't talk about it, but I knew my name was Salter and theirs was Jamison. Every time I had to write my name on a school paper or whenever I went to the doctor and she called me by my last name, I was reminded that I was different.

◆   ◆   ◆

It was in my seventh year with the Jamison Family that my social worker told me that my brother and I would be getting a permanent home soon. We would be moving from our long-term foster care placement to an adoptive home. I don't remember anyone explaining to us why we couldn't be adopted by the Jamison, but, then again, I didn't ask. I assumed that I was just too much trouble. Besides, I never seemed to fit in. *So what if they don't want me? I was going to get my own family. Maybe they'll even think I'm cute. Maybe I can stop being bad and they'll love me forever.* All of these thoughts went rushing through my head all at once.

My first question upon hearing the news was, "Will my name be the same as my new parents?"

"Yes, Shane," Mr. Pointer said.

I was ecstatic.

Due to our advanced ages, KB and I were classified as "hard to place." In most states, children age 18 months and older are deemed "hard to place" since hospital babies and infants are considered more desirable, adapt better and exhibit fewer abandonment issues. The fact that we were black and came as a package further decreased our chances of getting a good permanent home. For a fleeting moment, I wished I didn't have a brother. Maybe then, my chances would be better. Maybe people wouldn't compare me to him and talk about how cute he was all the time. However, in reality, my brother was my world. We were joined at the hip. I wouldn't go anywhere without him or ever leave him behind.

The recruitment process to find the best adoptive family moved very quickly after our photographs appeared in the *Amsterdam News*. I barely recognize the description of myself, even with the fictitious name:

> *"…Aside from being a very handsome looking, bright and creative young fellow, Sean loves singing and dancing and writing plays. He has a warm, outgoing personality, a good wit and is delightful company. He also makes friends easily once he gets to know you and has very little difficulty in relating to friendly adults. That's because he says, "I like people."*

When "advertising" for adoptive families, its common practice for agencies to give children fictitious names, but somehow KB's real name made it into print.

Amsterdam News - 1976

Sean and Keith

Sean And Keith:
An Adoptable Duo

Recently Sean, a 12-year old, was awarded a silver medal of honor for helping to rescue a baby from a fire. "And why not," says Sean, he goes on to say, "after all I'm a Boy Scout."

Having demonstrated such a remarkable act of courage and bravery, Sean and his nine year old brother, Kenneth are in need of an adoptive family as soon as possible. Especially a loving family who can provide a stable, secure and permanent home for them. One in which they can be very proud of knowing that someone willingly opened their home to them which they justly deserve.

Aside from being a very handsome looking, bright and creative young fellow, Sean loves singing and dancing and writing plays. He has a warm, outgoing personality, a good wit and is delightful company. He also makes friends easily once he gets to know you and has very little difficulty in relating to friendly adults. That's because he says, "I like people."

Sean and Kenneth have been a foster home for seven years which they thoroughly enjoyed and were made to feel an integral party of this family. Though the foster family agreed to care for them temporarily until a permanent home could be secured.

Due to their earlier life experience of being separated from their own family, one can imagine how painful and difficult it must be for them. That is, to miss out on the love that only a mother can give a child.

In spite of his good looks and unique sense of humor, Kenneth for the most part wears a bright smile and sports a "mischievous twinkle" in his eyes. Yet, he's so very affectionate when caught off guard. This doesn't imply that Kenneth is a "mommy's" boy, but he likes a hug every now and then to assure him that he's loved. In his spare time, Kenneth enjoys drawing but most of his energy is used in "hard play."

Sean and Kenneth would do well with a family who really want and need them. For more information on adopting these boys and other children like them, please contact the Adoption Department of Catholic Home Bureau, 1011 First Avenue New York, N.Y. 10022-tel. (212) 371-1000 ext. 370.

Several families responded to the newspaper article and eventually the most suitable family was selected. Eager to have a permanent home, I was determined to be on my best behavior. If I could be perfect, someone would finally want me and love me. I got the feeling that our new parents wanted me to be perfect, too.

During the pre-placement weekend visits, there always seemed to be so much excitement over our impending arrival. We were given everything we wanted. There seemed to be no limit to their generosity and kindness. A steady stream of relatives came by the house to meet us or we drove to their homes to meet our new grandparents, aunts, uncles and cousins. Introduced as the latest addition to the family, it was great getting all of the attention, and repeatedly hearing how handsome both KB and I were. A few relatives even commented on "the strong family resemblance."

On one particular visit, when Mr. Pointer, our social worker, dropped us off, he asked our soon-to-be parents when they would come to pick us up, and our new Dad's response was, "the twelfth of never." *How's that for having a real home and family? Our names will be the same as theirs. My dream is coming true: I will have a real family of my own, a place where I belong.* We finally had it made.

With "the twelfth of never" still ringing in my ears, I went back to the Jamison home confident and obnoxious in the belief that my turn had finally come. Not only was I going to be moving with a new family, they were rich, too.

I was angry with Mom and Dad Jamison for not adopting us. They never discussed their reason with us and I never asked. Since no one told me why my foster parents wouldn't adopt me, I told myself, "I'll show them that their rejection didn't matter to me. So what if they didn't want me."

After all, I reasoned, I was moving up in the world—going from an apartment in Crown Heights Brooklyn to a townhouse duplex in Co-Op City, The Bronx.

I danced around the house making up songs with words intended to hurt my foster family. "I'm so glad I'm leaving, because I'm going to a new home where people will love me forever." With each verse, I kept getting louder and louder to be sure that everybody in the house heard me clearly. This way, they wouldn't know that deep inside I felt rejected, scared, and lonely.

Once the paperwork was finalized, I really started acting out. A part of me really didn't want to leave what was familiar and safe. I didn't want to start all over again with another set of parents, a new set of rules, a new school and a new set of friends. I wasn't sure how well I'd adapt. Then there was part of me that looked forward to the new beginning, a chance to start all over again. I hoped these new people would understand me. I wanted to try, but wasn't sure I could hold up my end of the bargain. I didn't even know what the deal was.

Adoption was a new option for us and as I would learn sooner than later, I certainly didn't understand the rules of the game.

Because I did not understand why the Jamison were not keeping us, I wanted them to feel the pain I was feeling. However, I did not want to let them know I was mad and feeling rejected. I do not know if they ever knew how conflicted I was since I went out of my way to act as if I was happy to be leaving. Turns out my act was short-lived and about as convincing as one of my most transparent lies. Still I tried.

A few short weeks of boastful indifference and feigned happiness abruptly ended the day KB and I left the Jamison for good. We were finally being adopted. It should have been the happiest day of my life, but I cried and cried and cried.

"Mom, I don't want to go," I sobbed, hugging her as tight as I could. "Please mom, please."

My foster brother Robbie started crying too. I didn't even think he liked me. Why was he crying? He gets to have his parents all to himself, I thought. But when he hugged me and said goodbye, I knew it was real.

I looked up at Mom and Dad, and they were crying too. Why? I thought they wanted us to go. Mom Jamison never showed much affection, but at this moment, she held me and said, "You'll be okay, son."

She tried her best to put a positive face on things. "You've got a new family waiting for you and KB. Be good," she said, "And remember, we love you. The Robinsons will take good care of you and KB. You wait and see. You'll forget all about us after a while."

"No mommy," I wailed. "I'll never forget you, I promise."

We hugged, and I continued to cry uncontrollably.

"Don't let me go," I pleaded.

She just pushed me away.

"It's time, son," Dad Jamison said.

"No. No!" I screamed.

I grabbed KB, and the waiting adults grabbed me.

My instinct was to fight as hard as I could to stop them from taking me away. Suddenly, I surrendered. I didn't scream, scratch, kick, or bite. I took KB by the hand and let them lead us outside to the car waiting.

As we drove away, I wiped my eyes and thought about my new life and how wonderful this new family was going to be.

3

A FAMILY

o o o o o o o o o o o o o o o o o o o o o o o o o o o o o o o o o o o

when you look in my eyes, do you see?
a little boy wanting to be
love by a family
when you look at my face with no shame or disgrace
please remember, I'm just trying to run this race
trying to be
what I'd wish you'd see
a boy, who's a part of your family
oh what I'd do, if I could start a new, and rest among the chosen few
you see, I'd cry no more tears for the yesteryears, but I'd smile with joy
for the little boy, who became a part of your family.
S. Salter

When we arrived at our new adoptive home, the Robinsons were excited to see us. Mr. Robinsons worked for the Port Authority as a bus driver, and Mrs. Robinsons was a photographer and a beautician. She was a fox. They had one son named Anthony. Turns out Anthony saw our pictures in the *Amsterdam News* and begged his parents to let him have two brothers. On our absolute best behavior, we tried to behave like two model foster children. Everything in the article seemed to be as stated. KB and I were okay kids. Things were going really well, but a month after our arrival, the honeymoon ended and problems started to arise.

During the pre-placement visits, Anthony and I got along great, but as soon as we moved in, Anthony's resentment began to show. I guess he thought having brothers would be a lot more fun than being an only child. However, Anthony quickly learned that having two brothers meant sharing space, food, and his parents' attention. We would fight a lot about seconds at the dinner table. I think he was all right with sharing attention and living space but as big as he was (and I mean he was big), sharing food and eating less was out of the question.

We would fight over the pettiest nonsense whenever Mr. and Mrs. Robinsons weren't home. We would chase each other through the house with the rage of mortal enemies determined to fight to the death of one or the other of us. I was usually the one who picked up a stick. I wanted to beat him upside his head every chance I could get. I never could though. Anthony was no Robbie. He was a football player and he could fight. I wasn't used to that. He would wrestle me down or body-slam me once he caught me. When I lost a fight to Anthony, and I usually did, I would run to the closest pay phone and call Mom Jamison to complain and cry. I would tell her that I missed all of them and wanted to come back home.

Without fail and with incredible clarity, Mom Jamison would painfully remind me that the Robinsons were my family now, and that KB and I could never come back to live with her, Robbie and Dad Jamison.

"You got to make this work, Shane," she would say.

"But I'd rather live with you."

"You have a permanent home and a family that will adopt you. You have a new life now," she would remind me.

I'd hang up disappointed, but motivated to try to get along with Anthony, and stay out of trouble.

There were things that I liked about the Robinsons. They were much younger than Mom and Dad Jamison. Their house was cool too. Because Mrs. Robinsons was a photographer, I took an interest in photography, and they bought me my first camera. All my friends thought my new Mom was cool, too.

It didn't take long before I started making friends in my new neighborhood. I really hit it off with Todd, a taller, smooth, talking guy with curly hair that all the girls were crazy about. I thought Todd's single mom was so cool too, because she would often go out on dates, giving Todd and me time to get into all kinds of mischief.

One of my *favorite* neighborhood friends was a gorgeous Jamaican girl named Carmen. Man, was she hot. We would exchange notes and an occasional kiss when we passed one another in the hallways of the apartment building. One day, I got her to agree to skip school and go home with me. We got to the house and immediately got out of our clothes and started to have sex. Just as things were steaming up, my foster mom came home and caught us in my room. She screamed and told us to put our clothes on. That's when my real trouble began. She, of course, told Mr. Robinsons what I had done.

"Shane, I'm extremely disappointed in you. Not only have you tarnished the reputation of this family, but you've compromised the reputation of that girl and her family, too. I won't tolerate that kind of behavior in my house again. Do you hear me? I'm beginning to believe you can't be trusted to do what's expected of you." He was furious.

Although I pleaded with her not to, Mrs. Robinsons telephoned Carmen's parents and told them what we had done. Carmen's parents punished her by beating her terribly with an extension cord and forbidding her to ever speak to me again.

After I told Todd about the incident, it didn't take long for the news to spread. Everyone at school was talking about the fact that we were caught, which, ironically, made me more popular. I was now running neck and neck with Todd for the title of coolest dude in school because everyone knew I was getting my groove on with the girls.

After a week or so of being in the doghouse at home and having every privilege taken away, I started to feel that maybe I wasn't good enough to be a member of this family. My lying, stealing, and bedwetting increased. Then one day my whole world came to a screeching halt.

KB and I had been living with our new family for only about two months when my social worker, Mr. Pointer, unexpectedly made a visit to my school. I was called out of homeroom and told to report to the main office. As soon as I entered, my heart stopped. Mr. Pointer was standing at the counter waiting with a sad look on his face.

"We need to talk, Shane," he said as he led me back into the hallway. "The Robinsons called."

I immediately thought, "Oh, oh." I knew enough to know that his referring to them as "the Robinsons" instead of "your parents" was a bad omen.

"Things are not working out as they had hoped," he went on to say. "They want you and KB to leave."

I couldn't believe it.

"How long before we have to leave?" I struggled to get the words out. With no detectable show of emotion, he responded, "Tomorrow." "Tomorrow?"

Suddenly I was struck by lightening and my fragile heart was fried. It didn't seem to matter that I would turn 13 in a few days or that we had made plans to celebrate Thanksgiving as a family. In fact, no one seemed to mention it. I was crumbling, but couldn't move. All the hope and trust I placed in so many adults, adults who kept letting me go, passing me off, died as I leaned against the wall in that hallway. The wall was my tower of strength. For Sherry, Miss Fanny, Mom and Dad Jamison; a host of nameless adults working in the foster care system, my teachers, the nuns, none of them could save me from yet another set of parents who were sending us back. It felt like we were cargo with a stamp "Return to Sender." I would never trust again, I would never believe those three words "I love you." I went numb. I retreated to that dark blanket of fog and confusion. They *killed* the spirit of that little boy who so desperately wanted love and acceptance. The innocence was gone. My childhood snatched forever during that ten-minute conversation with Mr. Pointer.

"Mr. Pointer, why? Why don't they want me? Do adults ever mean what they say?" I asked, fighting back the tears as a new sense of rage welled up inside me.

"I thought they meant it when they said 'the twelfth of never. Even the shrink said adoption was permanent, so what happened? What did I do that was so terrible?"

Mr. Pointer tried to console me as best he could.

"Shane, you and KB will be okay," he said.

"Okay, Mr. Pointer? Okay?" I repeated, my voice rising. "What did I do that was so terrible? Tell me what I did? Where am I going to go?"

He quietly and calmly explained that KB and I would be going to an "emergency foster home" in the South Bronx. We were going to be moving from the somewhat upscale Co-Op City to a project in the South Bronx.

"Couldn't you find any place better than that?" I complained.

I would be returning to the place where I was born, so I knew it was going to be rough.

I told Mr. Pointer I needed to say good-bye to my friend before I left since this would be my last day at that school.

I couldn't leave without saying good-bye to Todd. I found him after school hanging out in the park. I told him that I was going to be moving away the next day. He was shocked when I told him that the Robinsons were not my real parents, that I was a foster child.

"My name really isn't Shane Robinson. It's Shane Salter," I confessed. "Man, stop lying. Why are you messing with me like that?"

When he realized I wasn't kidding, I could see a real sadness in his face. "Where are you going?" he asked.

"I don't really know, Todd. They tell me it's a family in the South Bronx," I said, as tears began to roll down my cheeks.

Todd tried his best to console me.

"Don't cry, Shane. We'll stay in touch. You'll still be living in the Bronx," he pointed out.

"Maybe I can come visit sometimes," I said.

◆　　　◆　　　◆

My next task was to tell my brother KB that we were going to have to leave yet another home. Just like me, I knew he really wanted this adoption to work. How could I break his heart again by telling him that the Robinsons wanted us to leave. I found him at home in our bedroom listening to Natalie Cole's "Good Morning Heartache." How ironic. "Hey, KB. I need to talk to you. It's important. I'm sorry, but we have to leave the Robinsons. Tomorrow Mr. Pointer is coming to get us," I told him.

"Why? They don't want us anymore?"

He looked as sad and confused as I had only hours earlier.

"Don't worry, little brother, we're going to be okay."

I didn't have a clue what "being okay" really meant. I only knew that the adults around me seemed to always say that whenever I was moving to another home. Therefore, that's what I told KB. He didn't know what "being okay" meant either.

That night, as we started to pack, I heard my soon-to-be ex-dad come in the house. A few minutes later, I went into his room to beg him not to send us back. Nothing I said seemed to change his mind.

"Shane, you created this situation. It's your fault that things didn't work out. You and KB have disrupted this family long enough. It's time for you to leave.

This has been a difficult time for us. I almost lost my wife once," he went on to say, "and I'm not going to let anyone or anything come between us again."

I fell on my knees crying and begging, "Please, Dad, don't send us back."

"Shane, it's too late. The decision has been made. Now go back to your room and finish packing."

Through the heartbreak, I mustered up the strength to tell myself I could handle whatever situation we might have to deal with in our "emergency" foster home. I was 12, but what about KB? I was really worried about him. He understood far less than I did. Now that I was back to being his parent again, I needed to find a way to comfort him, to reassure him, but all I could do was apologize.

"I'm sorry, KB, I'm so sorry."

I finished our packing and went to bed.

"Maybe they will change their minds by tomorrow," I thought.

When I awoke the next morning, my head seemed cloudy and I was overwhelmed with an incredible aloneness. I felt like an unwanted, motherless child, and that I was.

Of course, the Robinsons had not changed their minds. Our ex-parents placed our belongings and us in the car and drove very fast to the agency. The entire ride they kept saying the same thing over and over.

"You blew it, Shane. You blew a perfectly good home and family who loved" you.

Under my breath I mumbled, "If you really love me, why are you giving us back?"

"As long as you continue lying, stealing and wetting the bed you will never have a good home," Mr. Robinsons declared.

That car ride and their loud voices will be forever etched in my head. I couldn't see or hear anything else. It was like a bad dream. To make matters worse, when we pulled up in front of the foster care agency at 1011 First Avenue, they pulled us from the car, dumped us on the curb and sped away. There we were—KB and I—standing all alone with all our clothes in garbage bags. We just stood there for a minute looking at each other; then I took KB's hand and walked with him into the lobby of the huge 40-story office building.

I told the security guard seated in the lobby at the front desk who we were and what had just happened. He went back outside with us to retrieve our clothes, and after asking which agency we belonged to, he called someone from the Catholic Home Bureau and we were escorted upstairs. Right away, we were told about the next family we would be living with—a Mr. and Mrs. Bradford.

While we waited to be taken to the Bradfords, I made a decision not to steal from people anymore. As I saw it, the new foster home was another chance for a new beginning. No one had to know anything about my past, unless I told them or showed them. I didn't want to be known as a liar and a thief anymore. I didn't want people hiding their purses and wallets and talking about me behind my back. I couldn't handle that baggage anymore, not with everything else. I was no longer going to let my bad behavior prevent me from getting ahead. I wanted it gone. If it was going to stop me from getting a home, I wanted it gone. If it was going to stop me from reaching my dreams, as of that day…whatever it took, *it was gone.* Nothing and no one was ever going to say again that *I* was the reason holding me back.

Private transportation was arranged for our trip from Manhattan to the Bronx. The Bradfords lived in the Moore Housing Project on 149th Street in the South Bronx. The building didn't look so bad from the outside, but as soon as we got into the elevator, the stench of urine was so strong I almost passed out. I had to catch my breath. Going from the Jamison, to the Robinsons' beautiful townhouse, to the projects in the South Bronx was too much for me to handle. I tried not to walk in the apartment building with a bad attitude. I was grateful for having a place to stay. *Shoot,* after all, I had just been kicked out of somebody's house with my little brother and all, but…was this really, where we were going to be living?

I pretended, for the sake of my social worker, as if I didn't smell the weed when we walked into the lobby, but the pungent odor of urine was just outright nasty. Thank God, our new foster care mother lived on the fourth floor. As I got on the elevator, I was wondering what my social worker must be thinking. Would Mr. Pointer live here? Whatever his thoughts were, he kept them to himself.

A tall woman wearing a twisted wig and crooked glasses answered his knock. I stood there in disbelief. This can't be happening, I thought.

"Come on in," she says.

"Oh, no," I thought.

I was hoping she would say something more along the lines of "I'm sorry, but you obviously have the wrong apartment."

No such luck. I considered my options as she and my social worker chattered away. *Just tell me I get to register my own self for school. That is al I want to hear. I promise I'll get the best grades, if you promise never to show up at my school.*

The apartment was a dreary place; it had the distinction of being the first roach-infested apartment I had ever lived in. The sight of the place made me want to run back to the Jamison, but I couldn't. This was going to be my home now, and there was nothing I could do to change that. There were not a whole lot of options for two kids our ages. Natives of the Virgin Islands, with two grown children living elsewhere, the Bradfords were considered "professional" foster parents. Countless foster children had come in and out of their door, including one they had adopted permanently—Anthony, a kid about my age. Our status was clear from the outset. Mr. and Mrs. Bradford was not going to treat KB and I as well as they treated their adopted son, Anthony. I guess the underlying message was "Don't get too comfortable, you won't be here that long." Anthony went to Catholic school. KB and I were enrolled in a nearby public school. Anthony had his own room. KB and I shared one. All of the candy, cookies, and other goodies were locked up in the hallway closet. Anthony had the key. We didn't. It was without question his home and not ours.

We moved in with the Bradfords during the holiday season. I was really looking forward to a Christmas like the ones we had at the Jamison, with a tree and a living room filled with neatly wrapped presents. However, KB and I awoke on Christmas morning to find not one thing under the tree for us. Mrs. Bradford said that we came a little too late for her to get us anything.

"I do my Christmas shopping during the summer when prices are low," she explained.

At first, I thought she was joking, but she was dead serious. My brother and I just stared at each other. What did we do to deserve this? Wasn't it bad enough that my birthday was ruined?

I saw my therapist, Dr. Lewis, a lot more frequently during my stay with the Bradfords. During one particular visit in March, I had an experience that would change my life. The receptionist at the Catholic Home Bureau noticed that my last name was the same as that of a woman sitting in the reception area. Out of curiosity, she asked the woman if she knew a Shane and KB Salter. Well, not only did she know us, she said that we were here grandchildren!

When I arrived for my appointment a few minutes later, the receptionist grabbed me as soon as I got off the elevator.

"Shane, Shane, your grandmother is here!"

"What?" I inquired, completely puzzled.

I didn't know what to think because I had never met my grandmother. No one ever talked to me about her, and for some reason, with all the strong memories I had of my mother, she was not in any of them.

I was confused and nervous as the receptionist led me to a short, plump woman who stood up and said, "Shane, I'm your grandmother. And this is your sister," she said, pointing to the toddler standing beside her.

Shocked and elated, I hugged my grandmother, sinking happily into her soft bosom. It was the most comforting and sincere hug I had ever experienced. It seemed so real, so natural, and so right. Memories of my early childhood came flooding back and so did the unanswered questions that lingered all those years.

"Do I have a brother named Peter?" I asked.

"No, but you have an uncle who is only six years older than you named Pierre," she said.

"I remember him, Grandma, I remember him! All these years I thought he was my brother. We must have spent a lot of time together."

"You sure did, Shane," she confirmed.

I once thought my grandmother was a dark, thin, silver-haired woman with a Caribbean accent who used to feed me lots of red rice, and I told her. "Who is she, Grandma?"

"Oh, that's Ms. Turner, she was a sweet lady that lived in our building. She used to baby sit you."

I was so excited I was practically babbling now. "I remember the building I lived in, it had yellow brick and a fire escape outside the window."

She seemed genuinely impressed and shocked by how much I remembered.

Meanwhile, Mr. Pointer called the receptionist to ask if I had arrived for my appointment. That's when the receptionist casually mentioned that I was sitting in the lobby talking with my grandmother and sister. Well, I guess that meeting was not meant to happen because the next thing I knew, social workers were swooping in from every direction. They hustled me into one room and took my grandmother to another. Obviously, someone made a big mistake that caused my grandmother and me to be at the agency at the same time. They rushed me into a special session with my psychologist, Dr. Lewis, to help me "process" the experience.

She asked if I wanted to get to know my grandmother and sister.

"Of course," I replied.

"Okay, we'll see if we can arrange that," Dr. Lewis said.

Of course, I had a million questions. One of which would define the rest of my days.

"Where is my mother?" I had not forgotten her. I remembered her smell. I remembered her complexion. I remembered her songbird voice and how she used to sing to me. After all those years, I was still clinging to hope that someday Mom and I would be reunited.

I actually thought that my Mom was crazy and locked up in an institution somewhere. I reasoned that because I was seeing a shrink I was crazy, and that I probably inherited my craziness from her. However, she wasn't institutionalized. That's when Dr. Lewis told me my mother was dead. Neither one of us made a sound, I just sat there. We both just sat there and looked at each other.

Dr. Lewis knew what to expect; I didn't. My heart sank and a tear fell. I turned my head away and looked at the wall, staring at the play I'd written in elementary school and given to Dr. Lewis as a gift. She'd framed it and proudly displayed it after all this time. "The Adopted Child" was written when I still had hope of being with my mother again, and now that hope was gone. I would never be able to let her know that I was doing okay and that I would grow up strong and look after her just as I'd been looking after KB. I would never be able to ask why she never came back.

The only question I could ask Dr. Lewis was, "When is the funeral?" At least then, I would say my last good-bye.

At that point, Dr. Lewis reached from around her desk and took my hand.

"Shane, your mother died three months ago on December 16th We didn't tell you because it was less than a month after your adoption by the Robinsons fell through. We just didn't think you could handle the news at that time, you were going through so much."

"And I'm not now?" I sarcastically jabbed.

I was so hurt and angry.

"How could you let them keep that from me? Why didn't somebody tell me that my mother died? I should have been allowed to go to the funeral. No one had the right to withhold that kind of information. I only had one mother and I should have been able to say good-bye."

They'd stolen the one moment I had left to say good-bye, and I can never get it back.

◆   ◆   ◆

I went back to the Bradfords that afternoon sobbing bitterly to my foster mother of three months about all the news I had received that day. I was sad, confused, and angry. I desperately needed her to comfort me, to hold me, and to help make sense of all that happened that day. In a single afternoon, I met my grandmother, discovered I had a sister, and learned that my mother was dead.

Apparently, Mrs. Bradford decided that a scathing critique of my mother would help me more than the sympathy of a caring parent.

"You have no reason to cry about your mother's death because she never did anything for you anyway," she snapped. "If you all were my children, we would have survived off of bread and water and stayed together as a family."

I could not believe my ears. Her words crushed me, and left me not knowing what to feel. All I wanted was to be hugged, and made to feel, in that one moment, that I was not just a foster child, I was a human being in need of love, compassion and comforting. A mother other than my own had never held me, not even Mrs. Jamison. Why had I thought to confide in Mrs. Bradford? What was I setting myself up like that for anyway? *Shouldn't I have been used to comforting myself by now?* Never again.

A few days after meeting my grandmother for the first time, I learned that she had acquired the means to take care of KB and me and get us out of foster care! She had been offered a larger subsidized apartment with room enough for her, my sister, KB, and me. Words cannot express the horrible pain and disappointment I felt when I found out that she had refused the offer. She felt it was just too much, I was told. I was left to wonder, why? What was wrong with me? Maybe if I were just a little better behaved, just a little cuter, just a little smarter, maybe then she would want me. Maybe somebody would want me to be his or her kid.

It became painfully clear that all the time I had been separated from them that my family could have found me. They just didn't want to. Even with the offer of additional housing and resources, my Grandma did not want me. She could have taken the larger apartment, I thought, but she sent us back just like everyone else did. She could have at least tried it out for a while.

One day, about a year or so later, Grandma introduced me to a soft-spoken man with bright eyes. He was her dad. *Wow, this was my great—grandfather.* I couldn't believe I had a great-grandfather. All of my foster parents were old, you know, in their 40s, or older. I did not know that great-grandfathers really exist. What was most special about meeting him was something he said to me. He didn't just give me the standard "I'm so happy to see you. I remember when you were in diapers" line. I'd heard it enough times from family members and friends Grandma introduced me to and I quickly learned it had little or no meaning. They remembered me when I was in diapers because that's all they could remember.

Granddad on the other hand said, "Shane, I always thought about you. I hoped I'd live to see this day. Here," and he pulled out a white wrinkled little baby shoe with my name and birthday written in faded blue ink on the side, "I made your mother give me one of your first baby shoes when you were born because I knew, there was something special about you. See, you were born the night before President Kennedy was killed. The only baby born within that time at your hospital up there in the Bronx…"

"Wow you remember that, Granddad?" I excitedly responded.

"It was late night, and your mother almost died giving birth to you. In fact, she received her last rites."

He went on to say, "She was only 15 years old. They said she wasn't going to make it, but she did. She made it and you made it, but we lost a President the next afternoon. Don't you ever forget, now, that she also went to the Quonset Hut with your grandmother to have an abortion when they first found out she was pregnant with you. I'm not trying to start nothing, but your grandmother wanted her to finish her schooling. But somebody bigger than you and I had another plan. While lying on the table as they were getting ready to start the procedure, she jumped up suddenly and flew out of there."

He put his hand on my shoulder and looked me in the eye, and said "I didn't know then, and I don't know now, what you're destined to be, but I do know this, son, your life is destined for greatness." Then he went on to say,

"I have been saving this shoe for you all these years. Your mother would want you to have it, now that you and I have been reunited. Since all your baby pictures got lost in that awful fire several years ago, hold on to this shoe, it will keep you close to your mother, and remind you from where you came, and how great the struggle to get you here."

"Thanks, Granddad I will hold on to this forever." As chills raced up my spine.

Never could I have imagined a moment with my family so genuine and so tender. A humble man who had little material wealth embodied much of what had been eluding me in my foster care relationships: A belief in my potential. He let me know that I was valued, that I mattered.

My grandmother did agree to let KB and me come for occasional visits, but that did not last long. On one of my visits, my uncle's ring came up missing. Grandma was told that I had a history of stealing, and she immediately accused me of taking it. I couldn't believe it. I would never ruin my chance to have a relationship with my family by stealing from them. However, no matter how vehemently I insisted that I had not stolen the ring, Grandma wasn't hearing it. She forbade KB and me to come back to her house after that. A year later, she informed me that my uncle had misplaced the ring somewhere in the house, and that it had shown up a few days after she'd thrown us out. She could have told me sooner or at least made an effort to apologize, but she didn't. At the least, my name had been cleared. That was enough for me, but it wasn't nearly enough for KB. He was furious with Grandma for rejecting us again. He could not bring himself to tolerate a grandmother who would turn her back on her grandchildren. I tried to convince him to let it go, but he refused. Motivated by the desire to have a relationship with my sister, I was willing to put up with whatever I had to and to forgive whomever I needed to. I told myself, I don't care how she feels right now, I'm going to show all of them, everyone in my family, that like the Jennifer Holiday tune, "I'm Not Going.... *You're gonna love me.* "It may not be the love I need when I need it, but I'll show you through the strength of my character, I am not only worthy of your love, that I am, indeed, lovable and capable of loving. I kept working at and chasing this love as long as I could.

Learning of my mother's death and being rejected by my grandmother made me lonely, angry and sad for a while. I started having nightmares and became increasingly bitter towards my little brother. One night while he was asleep, I caught a roach and put it in his ear. It didn't go inside, it just crawled around the outside of the ear, but boy was it funny watching him jump out of bed screaming. When adults weren't looking, I would just slap or pinch him for no reason. I started resenting him and feeling that he was extra baggage. I was tired of looking after him. Looking after me was enough. I guess brown stuff rolls downhill; he was the only one I could take it out on. That is an unfair price to pay for being a little brother and I am sorry for my behavior toward him.

My life was getting to be more than I could handle. I started having bouts of wrenching, burning stomach pains that were caused by all the stress. Sometimes I'd be in such agony that I would lie in the bed biting my pillow so hard that I would tear the pillowcase. I told my foster mom yeah, that twisted wig woman with the crooked glasses but she didn't believe me. My brother would watch my suffering and cry. As mean as I had been to him at times, he still cared about me. One night he just couldn't stand it anymore, and he bolted out of the bedroom and went to our foster mom to tell her how much pain I was in. Mrs. Bradford simply dismissed him.

"There's nothing wrong with Shane, go back to your room," she said. Once again, I got no sympathy from Mrs. Bradford.

On several occasions, I had told my social worker, Mr. Pointer, about my stomach pains. He finally insisted that Mrs. Bradford have me evaluated by a doctor. It turns out that I was developing an ulcer. I took great pleasure in saying, "I told you so" to my foster mother, but she still refused to show any sensitivity toward me. Instead, she was just downright mean.

"Boy, go to your room. We all have pain. My knees have been hurting me forever and I've learned to live with it."

I hated her, and I hated living in that house! I never had enough to eat because Mrs. Bradford rationed our food. Fortunately, we were allowed to eat as much bread as we wanted, so I made toast all the time. When I put the bread in, the heat would make the roaches scatter from inside the toaster. It seems disgusting to me now, but I used to get such a kick out of watching the roaches scurry away. I ate so much toast in that house that anyone who knows me will tell you, I do not eat bread unless I am absolutely starving and there is nothing else in driving or walking distance.

I grew sadder with each passing day. Nothing seemed to be going right. I stopped smiling altogether because I simply had nothing to smile about. I became increasingly evil and rebellious. On several occasions, I slept on the subway riding from one end of the line to the other well into the night to avoid going home. Returning one night from an all-day subway ride, I knocked on the door and Mrs. Bradford let me in. I could tell that she had something hidden behind her, but I didn't know what. The next thing I knew she had hit me over the head with a big metal stirring spoon.

"What did you do that for?" I yelled.

I couldn't wait to find some kind of way to get out of that house. I did everything in my power to spend as little time there as possible. I continually came in after curfew just to keep from being at home.

I was 14 years old; deeply sad, extremely angry, and constantly getting into trouble. While playing outside one day, I was accosted by a neighborhood gang and forced to smoke my first cigarette. They told me that if I didn't try it, they were going to rub my face in the cement.

On another day, I found KB downstairs in front of our apartment building surrounded by a crowd of Latino boys that were about to jump him. I took on three to four of these boys at one time and won. After that, I was in constant danger of being jumped in retaliation, so I had to find a place to lie low for a while. Eventually, I found sanctuary in a dollar movie theater down the street that used to show Bruce Lee flicks and other old movies. It was not unusual to see strange men in the theatre's bathroom masturbating at the urinals. While I was using the bathroom one day, a man standing next to me offered me money if I would leave with him. Oblivious to the danger, I followed him to his car. He unzipped my pants, fondled me, and masturbated. When he was done, he gave me lots of money and drove me back to the theater. I walked to my foster home feeling really confused. Why had I let that happen to me? I really needed someone to help me make sense of it, but I certainly wasn't going to talk to Mrs. Bradford about it.

I eventually started making friends in the Bradfords' building. Having friends helped me handle living in the house a little better. Two of my best friends were Robert and his sister Daphine. They were foster kids like me. Their apartment had carpet and furniture with plastic slipcovers just like the Jamison'. Their foster mother, Mrs. Boxale, was the sweetest woman in the world. I was jealous. Man, why didn't I get a foster home like this one? Every time I went upstairs to their apartment, I asked Mrs. Barksdale if there was any way KB and I could live with them. Besides having a much nicer home and decent parents, I liked the idea of living under the same roof with Daphine. I was very attracted to her, and before long, she was my girlfriend. Daphine, Robert and I played upstairs in their room and had lots of fun as often as we could. For me the Barksdale house was a safe refuge, a home away from hell.

Robert and Daphine's foster parents had a cousin named Joseph. He was in his early twenties, recently discharged from the Marines, and on a fast track as an executive at the telephone company. Joe often came by the house to see Daphine and Roberts' older foster brother and sister, the Boxale's birth children. The Boxale's told Joe about how badly the Bradford's were treating me and how unhappy I was. He took an interest in me and took it upon himself to be a big brother to me. Joe spent a lot of time coaching me through my problems and encouraging me to be strong. Sometimes that "be strong" stuff made me mad. How I can be strong, I would think to myself. I have no one.

Joe helped me realize that I had no other choice; that there was no other option. He had no tolerance for whining. He reminded me frequently that I was smart and that my only chance to change the direction of my life was through education.

"You have to finish school," he always said. "That's what matters most."

I knew what Joe was saying was true, but it wasn't that simple. I had so much on my mind all the time. It was just too hard to concentrate in school. How was I supposed to concentrate on schoolwork when I was hopeless, hungry, and homeless? For me school was just another place where I didn't fit in and where no one seemed to understand me. Most of the time I fantasized during classes about a life much better than the one I was living, a life where I was actually loved and encouraged to be myself. I was getting so tired of putting on an act in order to fit in, but strangely enough, I was getting good at it.

Joseph drove a sharp navy-blue Chrysler, had a nice apartment, and had many well-established friends. Hanging around him exposed me to successful people and a standard of living I had not seen before. They became my role models. I wanted to be just like them. I got along much better with them than I did with people my age. Eventually the things Joe said started sinking in. I started thinking, if I want nice things like he has, maybe I should take his advice. He was a great father to his little girl and I really admired that. Joe made me feel as if I mattered; he always kept his word, and showed up when he promised. I looked up to him. At a time when my life could have gone in any direction, his interest in me was like a bridge over troubled water. More importantly, he taught me that the best way to crossover troubled water is to count on no one, and develop the tools necessary to build my own bridges. He kept drilling in my head however; that you will always be at the mercy of others if you do not have your own tools. By tools, he was talking about education, communication skills, and experience. What he said was true largely, but I later learned, you do have to know how to depend on people every now and then during times of trouble. You just have to hope they really got your back and will show up when you need them.

◆   ◆   ◆

It was a cold and very sad day when the news broke that Mrs. Boxale had a sudden heart attack and died. Stunned, I ran upstairs to find Daphine and Robert. As we hugged each other, Robert said, "I don't know what's going to happen to us now."

I started to cry, and all I could say was, "It'll be all right."

The morning of the funeral, it still seemed like a bad dream. The limousine and hearse were parked outside the building. Joe and the funeral directors led us downstairs for the processional to the church. I remember Joe whispering to me, "Keep it together. Don't go making no performance."

"What did he mean by that?" I remember thinking. Was I not supposed to cry? Why was I always being told to mask my emotions?

A few days later, Daphine and Robert were moved to another foster care home. I never saw them again.

It wasn't too long afterwards that during one routine visit with our social worker, Mr. Pointer, he asked KB and me if we were ready to move out of Mrs. Bradford's house. In unison and without a moment of hesitation, we both said "Yes."

"How does living in a group home sound?" he asked.

Everything I knew about life in a group home I learned from watching "Fish," a popular television sitcom at the time. The kids on the show seemed to have a lot of fun, so we agreed. There was, however, one condition—KB and I would be separated. They couldn't send siblings to the same group home. Surprisingly, the thought of being separated was not a big deal to either of us. We were getting tired of each other anyway, or so we thought. With all the years of brotherly fights and sharing rooms and stuff, we thought it would be good not to be around each other for a while. I know I was tired of having him around. Carrying him was a heavy burden. I needed to be free for a while from the responsibility of looking after the two of us. I needed time to look out for myself, to be on my own for a while.

4

SOMEDAY

o o o o o o o o o o o o o o o o o o o o o o o o o o o o o o o o o o

Keep on walking tall, hold your head up high
Lay your dreams right up to the sky
Sing your greatest song
and you'll keep going on
Take it from me; someday we'll all be free....
A. Keyes

My little brother KB and I moved into separate group homes.

I moved into a large group home on Lacombe Avenue in the Soundview section of the Bronx. Mr. and Mrs. Hopkins, the house parents, lived in an apartment upstairs during the week and drove to their house in Connecticut on weekends. The kitchen refrigerators had steel doors that were locked unless meals were being prepared. The home had a diverse mix of children, including some in wheelchairs. That was hard to get used to at first, but I quickly realized that despite our differences, we all had a lot in common. They had the same hopes and fears that I did. They wanted to be happy, just like I did. They were misunderstood, just as I had been. And just like me, someone had rejected them too.

I'll always remember Eric. A resident of the home, he had been born with no arms or legs. I made the *mistake* once of mouthing off to him. I thought, if there's anyone I should be able to mouth off to and get away with, it would be the kid in the house with no arms and legs. *Eric taught me a lesson or two.* Dude hopped out of his wheelchair onto the floor faster than a speeding bullet. He picked me up with one of his upper stubs, threw me to the floor, and whipped my butt with the other stub. I didn't know what hit me, literally. He quickly earned my respect. I had to learn what everyone in the house already knew, don't mess with Eric. There's more strength in those short stubs than most of us have in our arms.

Another person who taught me a thing or two was Eugene. He was also in a wheelchair. We became very close friends. Eugene, who had cerebral palsy, was one of the smartest and most compassionate people I had ever met. He was like a brother to me.

In fact, there was a bond among all the kids in the house that transcended ethnicity or disability. This home was different from any I had ever lived in.

There was one thing, unfortunately, that being in a new home had not changed: I still found a way to get into a tremendous amount of trouble. Some of the guys and I would take Eric on the train in his wheelchair. Grasping a can between his stubs, he would beg passengers for money. At the end of the day, we would equally split everything we collected. And boy would we clean up!

It was also the time in my life when I started experimenting with weed, beer, and cigarettes. Hanging out with the boys one night, I put down a quart of Olde English, smoked a joint and my first Salem cigarette. My head was spinning so badly, my stomach so upset, that I thought I was going to die. When I came back to the group home, I tried to lie down but the room kept spinning. I promised myself that if I lived through the night I would never do that again. When I woke up the next morning, I found myself on restriction—a group home term for punishment—for two weeks. Regrettably, it did not deter me. My desire to fit in with the boys was much greater than my fear of being punished. I just figured I would smoke and drink a little less the next time around.

During my stay at the Soundview Group Home, I was diagnosed with Grand Mal Epileptic seizures. I couldn't believe it. I'd already been through hell in my short fourteen-year life. Now my body was under attack by these seizures that seemed to come upon me without warning and for no apparent reason. I was angry and depressed. The last thing I wanted was another challenge in my life, and here I was with epilepsy. Something else to make me feel like a freak. The doctors put me on dilantin and phenobarbital to bring the seizures under control. As much as I could, I ignored the seizures and went on with my life. Seizures went on uncontrollably until my junior year of high school. Just as the abnormal EEGs appeared, they were replaced by consecutive normal ones and the seizures just went away.

It was at Soundview that I met one of my best female friends ever. Vanessa was kind and loving, but also no nonsense. She was just as tough as she was kind and would kick your butt in a minute. We never dated or anything, but Vanessa and I developed an extremely close friendship. Vanessa introduced me to her parents, Mr. and Mrs. Morkges. I grew to like them so much and Vanessa and I were so close that I asked Vanessa if I could live with her family. I was so disappointed when they said I couldn't, but we all remained very close, and Vanessa and I started referring to each other as brother and sister.

I had been attending the New York School of Printing High School for about a year when I auditioned for the theater program at Julia Richman High School for the Performing Arts. I was determined to fulfill my dream of becoming an actor so I could show all those people who did not want me that I was special. I knew I had an acting gift and, that it just might be a way out of my seemingly inescapable childhood pain of loneliness and rejection. I jumped, screamed and ran up and down the stairs the day I got my acceptance letter to Julia Richman. There was no doubt in my mind that I was destined to be a great movie star. Becoming a student at this highly regarded school was the first step toward fulfilling that dream. Every day was a great day at Julia Richman. I worked hard in my acting classes, determined to perfect my craft. One of the most exciting moments from that period of my life was when MGM studios held auditions at our school for the movie "Fame." I auditioned for the part of Leroy, and I must have really impressed MGM because I got a callback. However, I guess it just was not my time. The part of Leroy went to one of my school rivals, Gene Anthony Ray. Gene was an awesome dancer with a nasty attitude, but, to me, he could not act.

Therefore, with him as my main competition for the role, I just knew I was going to get it. Obviously, they wanted a dancer, not an actor.

At the movie's premier, I was sick with envy. I could not help but wonder what my life might be like if I was up on that movie screen playing Leroy instead of Gene. "Fame" had taken Gene out of the hood to the kind of life I wanted so badly. For me, it was back to the hood and living in the group home. It was not very long after that, though, that I got a different kind of ticket out of the hood. The social workers had identified another adoptive family for me. It would be in Rochester, New York with an unmarried Baptist minister.

◆   ◆   ◆

Reverend Kennedy had already successfully adopted a six-year-old boy. That record of accomplishment gave me hope that perhaps this time an adoption would finally work for KB and me. However, KB wanted no part of family living again. The thought of being with a family again and being rejected was just too painful. The Jamison let him down and the Robinsons had suddenly tossed us aside after two months. Group-home living, without any emotional attachments and ties, was safer, he decided. However, I saw this as an opportunity for us to be reunited and a chance for me to take care of him the way I used too. I knew he needed me.

While we were separated, KB's behavior was getting bad. He started stealing bicycles and getting into all kinds of trouble. No one could get through to him. The social workers kept calling me to talk to KB about his behavior because I was the only one he would listen to. That's why I didn't want to pass up the chance for this adoption. I didn't even care that Rochester was so far away from New York City; maybe that was a good thing. It seemed that I had experienced nothing but pain in the Big Apple anyway. So I took charge of the situation and told KB that we were going to do this whether he wanted to or not. It was a chance for us to be loved, happy, and secure. Besides, we had started to miss living with each other, and deep down I know he wanted to be with his big brother. He must have known that I would find a way for us to be together again, and this was it.

In my mind, being adopted and having a family was the absolute answer to all of my troubles. I dreamed constantly of living in a big house, having a nice car, and wearing nice clothes. It hurt so much whenever I would hear other children talk about their parents. It did not matter whether what they said about them was good or bad, at least they had parents. I wanted my own mom and dad. Besides, it was my job to protect KB. A family meant security, and if anything ever happed to me, he would be safe with them. I realized that the clock was running out for us because we were no longer two cuddly little boys in need of a home. We were teenagers now, and people were not knocking down doors to take in kids like us. That's why on the day we met with Reverend Kennedy for the first time, I whispered to KB, "Look, man, don't blow it. Smile a lot," I advised him. "We have to be on our best behavior."

It worked! After a few visits, we were leaving the past behind and moving out of New York City to Rochester. I had another chance at my lifelong dream of having a family we could call our own.

Once again, we were starting fresh with a new home and a new dad. I decided that I wanted to mark the new beginning by changing my name. Somehow, I reasoned that the name Shane had only brought me and everyone else around me heartache. My new dad's only stipulation was that I had to research the meaning of my new name and write a full page explaining why I chose it. I picked the name Karim, which means "generous." My full name became Karim Abdu Jamar Kennedy. KB decided to just change his middle name from Earl to KB.

At our new home, I was excited to have a new little brother, who my new dad had also adopted. His name was Marcus, and we hit it off immediately. I think KB was a little jealous of him, but at the same time, he seemed happy to finally be a big brother. KB would attend the same school as Marcus—St. Louis Catholic School in Pittsford, New York. My new dad took me on site visits to choose a school. We visited two public high schools, one all-boys Catholic school, and one co-ed Catholic school. After touring and meeting with principals of all four schools, he asked me to rate them in order of my preference. I thought it was so cool that he was going to let me choose. Eager to exercise this wonderful new freedom, I quickly rated the two public high schools one and two, the Catholic co-ed school number three, and the all-boys Catholic school last. I turned my preferences over to Dad, who looked at them and said, "You will be attending St. Thomas Aquinas."

It was the most academically rigorous of the four and the one with no girls. I wanted to know why he had bothered to ask my opinion only to select the one I chose as my last preference. He said that St. Thomas Aquinas would be the most challenging, and he thought black boys needed academic challenges to prepare them for manhood. Then my dad hit me with the biggie. He told me that I would start this new school in the ninth grade, although New York City Public Schools (NYCPS) had duly promoted me to the tenth grade. He said he had no confidence in the NYCPS curriculum because the standards were inferior.

Okay, I admit my grades sucked. I *was* passing, even though it was with C's and D's.

My attitude towards Reverend Kennedy changed. Who was this big, fat, afro wearing dude to come into my life and tell my school to make me repeat a grade? As if that was not bad enough, I had to cut off my long-awaited mustache because the school did not allow boys to have facial hair. From that moment on, I was convinced he was a bona fide butt hole. All of a sudden, group home living looked like paradise. At least there, I was able to make my own decisions.

There was no changing my dad's mind about how things were going to be. I was enrolled at predominantly white St. Thomas Aquinas. I made friends quickly, especially with the few black kids that were there. All of them came from very good homes with strong values. They followed the rules, did their homework on time, and stayed out of trouble. One kid stood out from the others. He appeared unhappy and angry, and acted as if he did not want to be there. He was a notorious "bad boy" at school, so, naturally, I wanted to be friends with him. I was actually afraid of him until we discovered that we had so much in common. Neither of us was living with our parents and Kevin's parents were struggling with substance abuse like the one my mother had. Kevin and I were drawn to each other and hit it off right from the start. Meeting him was like a ray of sunshine coming through prison bars.

I started to feel like a prisoner living with my new dad. He actually screened my letters from my grandmother, my friend Vanessa, her parents the Moorages' and other folks from New York City. He forbade me from remaining in contact with my family and New York friends. He said it was out of concern for the kind of influence they might have over me while I was adjusting to my new home. I didn't understand his rationale. I was mad, and felt cut off from the world I'd known all of my life. The more he tried to make me forget my past, the more I longed to hold on to it.

With Dad's permission, I decided to join the school band.

"What instrument do you want to play?" Dad asked.

"The teacher said he only has space in the percussion section, so I could either play the drums or the xylophone."

"I didn't ask you what the band instructor said. I asked *you* what instrument *you* want to play."

"I've always wanted to play the trombone."

"Then that's what you'll play." he declared.

As he drove me to the music shop that night, I wondered how I was going to just show up at school with a trombone when the teacher had said there was only room in the percussion section.

The next day, Dad went to school with me, and spoke privately with the band teacher. I don't know what he said, but I played the trombone in the band that year. Now that was cool. I never had anyone go to bat for me like that before. I never mattered like that to anyone. "Is this what it means to be somebody's kid?" I wondered. "Is this what real parents do for their children?" All I knew for sure was that, at that moment, I felt special.

On another occasion, the school sent a note home indicating that, in accordance with the rules, I had to shave my little peach fuzz of a mustache off. Once again, my dad stood up for me, and I became one of the only kids in school who didn't have to shave. In my eyes, Dad had more than redeemed himself. I was beginning to dig this family thing again.

Meanwhile, KB and I worked at getting used to living with each other again. Being under the same roof, we started having fights over some of the pettiest of things. One Sunday after church, I flew into a rage over socks. I noticed that my white tube socks were damaged beyond repair.

"No matter how many times I tell KB not to wear my clothes he never listens," I fumed. "Dad doesn't do anything to KB when he does something wrong," I recalled. "KB just does whatever he wants."

After a few minutes of egging myself on, I was furious, and before I knew it, I was screaming at the top of my lungs, *"I'm so sick of this shit."*

I'm not sure if it was the fact that I cursed, or the fact that I cursed on a Sunday, but my dad must have been on his way to the kitchen before the words were out of my mouth. He came flying into the room and slapped me upside my head. Shocked, angry, and extremely embarrassed, I ran upstairs and locked myself in my room. I lay across the bed for what seemed like hours, growing more distraught about my life with every minute. "This adoption is going down the tubes fast," I decided. "They always like KB better than me," I thought. I reached the conclusion that I couldn't do anything right.

I decided that the best course of action was to kill myself. I looked at my dilantin, and without hesitation swallowed all of the pills. As I sat on my bed, my eyes got heavy, and I became extremely groggy. Convinced that I was on my way to certain death, I reconsidered and stumbled downstairs to tell Dad what I had done. He hustled KB, Marcus, and me into the car and rushed to the hospital. The emergency room physician chastised me for trying to take my life.

"Nothing could be that bad," he said. "Oh yes it could" I mumbled under my breath. "Living with my dad is hell."

As they were getting the pills out of my system, I overheard Dad say to the doctors and nurses that he wanted this to be a miserable and unforgettable experience for me. Against medical advice, he signed me out of the hospital. On the way home, he stopped at a steak house and parked the car near the kitchen where I could fully experience the nauseating aroma of food cooking.

The next morning, despite being at the hospital extremely late, Dad woke me up bright and early for school. When we arrived at school, he walked me into the principal's office and issued clear instructions to the faculty that I was to attend all classes regardless of how I felt. Although the school usually respected his wishes, when they learned what I'd been through the night before, they let me go to the guidance counselor's office, where I slept most of the day. I felt vindicated. Even the school felt Dad was being unreasonable. In my mind, the same father who had made me feel special by standing up for me had now turned completely against me. "Okay, I get the message," I thought. "Maybe attempting to kill myself is something I'll think twice about next time. But if this mental anguish keeps up, I'll finish what I started."

My dad's unconventional perspective started making me unpopular at school. After a few weeks of checking my homework, he decided that I wasn't bringing home a sufficient amount. "Oh, this won't work," he said. "I'll have to let them know that I'm paying too much tuition for them to be sending this nonsense home and calling it homework."

And that's exactly what he did. As a result, the homework load for the entire class doubled, and somehow it got out that this was as a direct result of my dad's actions. I caught much grief from the entire class, including my boy Kevin.

When Dad found out that I was friends with "bad boy" Kevin, he told me not to associate with him during school so I could fully focus on my academic priorities. Kevin and I started talking on the phone late into the night to compensate for the fact that we couldn't talk at school anymore. One night we talked until 2 a.m. about everything from sex to drugs, not knowing that my dad was eavesdropping.

The next morning all hell broke loose. Dad jumped all over me and forbade me to have any contact with Kevin ever again. He even asked Kevin's grandmother to help him enforce his new rule, but, fortunately, she ignored him and continued to let me hang out with Kevin at her place. With each day that passed, I was growing more and more resentful of Dad. If this was what having a father meant, then maybe I didn't need one.

When the nearby all-girls school partnered with our all boys school to have a dance, Dad insisted on meeting my date beforehand. Before I could call someone a friend, he had to approve. The night of the dance, my date's parents dropped her off at my house where I introduced her to Dad. Well, she seemed to pass inspection because he allowed us to leave for the dance without any objections. After I got home from a fantastic evening, Dad said that he disapproved of my date because she didn't stand up to greet him. "How ridiculous," I thought. Living with this man was just getting to be too much.

My resentment towards my dad continued to grow. I started complaining about him to anyone who'd listen. Even the adults I confided in agreed that he was simply too unreasonable.

Finally, I decided it was time to get away from Reverend Kennedy for good. I ran away to Kevin's house with no intention of ever returning. Regrettably, that was the first place Dad looked for me, and he had me back home in a matter of a few hours. I ran away several more times after that, and each time Dad would call the same big black police officer to fetch me home.

Determined to finally run away and not to be caught, I saved enough money to get a bus ticket back to New York City. I had several hours before my bus was scheduled to leave, so I called Dad's mother, Grandma Kennedy. She asked me where I was, but I wouldn't tell her, fearing she'd blab to Dad. She told me that she felt badly about how unreasonable my father was being. After implying that she understood what I was going through, my defenses were lowered by her empathy. Somehow, I really did think I could trust her. I told her where I was and she offered to take me to her place to get some sleep before I got on the bus the next morning. On the way to her house, Grandma stopped by Dad's house "just to get your pajamas," she promised.

She had me duck down in the back seat so Dad couldn't see me. She retrieved the pajamas, and we were on our way. About thirty minutes after arriving at Grandma's, the doorbell rang. To my surprise, it was Dad and the same police officer who had chased me down so many times before.

"Shane, don't you think I have anything better to do other than chase you around Rochester?" the officer quipped.

"As long as you keep sending me back to his house, you are going to have to keep chasing me," I shot back.

Little did I know; I would not be going back to my dad's house.

They took me to a place called Hillside Children's Center. It was a cold place with heavy metal doors that locked tight behind me as I entered the building. They told me that I would be staying at Hillside for two weeks and that Dad was forbidden to see me while counselors helped me work out my problems. At the end of the two weeks, a Rochester social worker and my social worker from New York City, Mr. Pointer, met with my dad and me. They asked if I wanted to go back to Dad's house. I quickly responded with a firm "NO." They said that Dad wanted me home and was willing to change some of his parenting techniques.

"Yeah, he might change, but I doubt it," I thought. I didn't want to take that chance. I told them that there was no way I would ever go back. I looked up and was shocked to see a tear fall from my dad's eye. Seeing him cry for the first time made me think about staying with him, but I couldn't give in. I just couldn't. In fact, a part of me wanted to cause him as much pain as I could.

I looked him straight in the eye and spoke words that I hoped would hurt him as all my parents before him had hurt me.

"I'm 15, and you're 25. What makes you think you can ever be my father?" Everyone stared at me in disbelief. I just stared right back, determined not to display any trace of sadness.

"Reverend Kennedy is willing to keep your brother KB whether you stay or not" someone said.

"If KB has a chance to have a family, That's great. No problem, then I am not going to stand in the way." I responded. Besides, KB was not having the same problems I was. He was a good kid. Then Dad said something that truly pierced my heart.

"If you leave, there's no coming back. *And* you can never see or talk to KB again."

Swallowing an orange-size lump in my throat, I looked at him and everyone else in the room and said, "If that's what it takes, no problem."

Tears fell down my face as the magnitude of my decision sunk in. I had agreed to leave my brother behind, which meant leaving my heart and a piece of soul behind. Without KB, what was my purpose for living? At least I had accomplished my life task as his parent. He was safe. He had a family. Perhaps I was a bad influence on him. Maybe KB would be better off without me. I needed to focus on getting my life straight now. At that moment, I accepted the reality that my dream of having a family would never materialize.

It made me sad, but I knew it was true. It was time to go. I declared that there would be no more trying to hit targets that kept moving. No more trying to be cute enough to win over families or behaving well enough not to be kicked out of one. I realized some dreams just could not be. From that moment on, I knew I was all that I had, and I was determined to survive.

My eyes were red and swollen from crying by now, but Mr. Pointer knew my mind was made up.

"Well, Shane, how do you want to travel back to New York City?" "I've never been on a plane before," I confessed, my voice quivering.

Doing his best to console me and lift my spirits, he said, "Then let's fly back, Shane."

And so we did.

Once again, Mr. Pointer was there to help me pick up the broken pieces of my life. Mr. Pointer was more than a social worker to me. He was like family. It was obvious from day one that he really cared about me. I never felt like he was just a social worker. For some odd reason, he thought I had potential. He really believed in me and believed me. I could see him out of the corner of my eye, when I was sad; he would be standing to the side, fighting back tears. It was strange. I never had a black male social worker before. He was also a tough no-nonsense guy, so I never quite figured out how to manipulate him. Mr. Pointer only gave me but so much rope before yanking it back.

The flight from Rochester to New York City was my first airplane ride. It was very exciting. But I thought it was sad, though, that Mr. Pointer didn't have a place for me to stay when I returned to New York City. He asked me if I had any ideas.

"How about the Moorages?" I suggested.

"Why don't you call them and see if they would be willing to be an emergency foster home for you.

I called Vanessa and she asked her Mom and Dad, who promptly agreed to take me in for a while. They had never liked Reverend Kennedy anyway.

5

A DREAM WITH YOUR NAME ON IT

o o o o o o o o o o o o o o o o o o o o o o o o o o o o o o o o o

Stand tall, don't you be afraid,
you're sure to find your way, when that voice that's deep inside
you, says to take a chance—
that's what you have to do, Follow your heart—go where it
leads you. It's telling you—there's a dream out there with
your name on it.
J. Holiday

Back in New York City...

I was determined to make the most of my life. I had two failed adoptive place-
ments under my belt, and there was something I wanted to prove to myself and
to all those who repeatedly said I'd never be anything. Fortunately, the Moorages
were willing to give me a place to stay while Mr. Pointer and I sorted things out.
The Moorages lived in Mitchell Houses, another public housing development. It
was actually one of the better ones. I didn't smell urine in the elevators as much
as I had in some of the others, and at least it wasn't roach infested.

My return to New York was emotionally difficult for me. I had just been separated from my brother again, and had to accept that I would never see or speak to
him anymore. My seizures started coming with greater frequency and intensity. I
was in and out of the hospital all the time. At one point, they were occurring with
such frequency; the neurologist expressed serious concern about the effect on my
nervous system. It was obvious what was happening. KB was living with the man
who I wanted so desperately to be our father, and keep us together. I was grieving
for my brother and the lost relationship with a father as if they had both died. I
would not have made it through all that without Pop Moorages. He and I really
connected, and his presence had a comforting and calming influence on me.

While the social workers were completing the paperwork for the Moorages to
become my long-term foster parents, doctors discovered that Mom Moorages
had been exposed to TB. That meant I had to be immediately removed from
their home. Thanks to a positive TB test, I was going to have to leave a place
where I finally felt comfortable and had been accepted unconditionally.

"This can't be happening," I groaned.

I was beginning to think I shouldn't have bothered to unpack; whenever I
moved some place new, I was never there long. I hated having to leave the Moorages. But, I had no choice.

Mr. Pointer was able to find yet another foster family for me, this time in the
Bushwick section of Brooklyn. Mr. and Mrs. Eberlys had a son and a daughter.
They also had a teenage foster child named Fritz living with them. It was clear
from the very beginning that they planned to adopt Fritz and that they had no
interest in adopting me. What foster parent wouldn't have wanted to adopt Fritz?
He was easygoing, didn't talk back, and helped around the house. The closest
thing he had to a vice was an occasional basketball game. I, unfortunately, was
nothing like Fritz.

Mr. and Mrs. Eberlys were devout Roman Catholics. The house was filled
with statues of Mary, Jesus, and Joseph. There was a strong Muslim community
in the neighborhood as well. Although I was growing up under the supervision of

a Catholic agency and I'd had strong Catholic influences from the Jamison Family; I was always impressed and intrigued by Muslims. They were so neatly dressed and seemed so disciplined. I started thinking that maybe that was what was missing in my life: self-discipline. Maybe if I were more disciplined I could focus better in school, and if I focused in school like my big brother Joe said, I would achieve my goals. I started paying a lot more attention to the Muslims—the way the women only revealed their eyes and the men draped themselves in clothing from head to toe. When a man's head was exposed, he always had a very neat close-tapered haircut. To me, they stood out and represented themselves well.

On my way home one day, I stopped into the neighborhood mosque, talked with some of the brothers there, and decided to have my Shahada (the equivalent of Christian baptism). I selected a Muslim name, which was Elijah Abdullah Kareem Abdula Muhammad (EAKAM for short). I told the brothers of the Ansar Allah Community that I was homeless. I had a place to sleep with a foster family, but it wasn't really home for me. I told them that the Catholic Home Bureau was my guardian and that none of the homes they found for me had worked out. I asked the brothers if they would adopt me and let me grow up as a Muslim. The brothers welcomed me. They said they were willing to adopt me and that they would be happy to have my social worker visit their community to determine if it was a suitable place for me to live. They even said they would send me to college if my grades were good enough, but they would decide my field of study based on the needs of their community. That probably meant my career in theater was out of the question. However, for what I'd get in return—safety, security, discipline, and a permanent home—I thought it was a good tradeoff. Besides, I had felt drawn to the Muslims for quite some time. I was sure that this was the right place for me.

I returned to Mrs. Eberlys that day dressed as a new Muslim wearing all white with my kufi, feeling euphoric. When Mrs. Eberlys opened the door, she looked as if she had seen a ghost. She pulled herself together long enough to ask, "Did any of the neighbors see you coming down the street?" She seemed quite frazzled. Apparently, the sight of me in Muslim clothing had sent her over the edge.

"I can't take any more of this; they're going to have to do something with you. I can't have you around here dressed like that," she complained.

She phoned Mr. Pointer and told him that I had to go immediately. I don't know what Mr. Pointer said, but she calmed down and handed me the phone. I told Mr. Pointer that I had asked the Muslims to adopt me, and that they said they would. He immediately set up an appointment to visit the mosque.

I don't know what happened during Mr. Pointer's visit to the Ansar Allah Community, but it definitely made an impact on him. He told me that if I ever went back there I would be sent straight to juvenile hall. I supposed he thought that would be the end of it, but I refused to accept his decision. I knew enough to know that I had the constitutional right to practice the religion of my choice. Therefore, I called the New York Legal Aid Society for help. I explained to the woman who answered the phone that I was a foster child under the guardianship of the Catholic Home Bureau, and that I had just become a Muslim.

"Don't I have a constitutional right to freedom of religion?" I demanded to know.

I could not have been more disappointed when she told me that as long as I was a ward of the state, the state was my guardian, and I had to do what they said. I could practice whatever religion I wanted, she said, when I turned 18. That's when it hit me: I was the property of New York State. That meant that the state controlled my every move, and it meant that I had to accept what Mr. Pointer said.

I never went back to the mosque again.

Thankfully, Mrs. Eberlys got over being upset that I had become a Muslim and decided to allow me to remain in their home until other arrangements could be made for me. I was happy to have a place to stay, but what I really wanted was to be out of foster care, on my own, and making my own decisions. The decisions other people were making for me just seemed to screw up my life. I was sure I could do better. However, that would have to wait. For now, it was back to foster care at the Eberlys.

The Eberlys' Bushwick neighborhood wasn't a very safe part of Brooklyn. In retrospect, I probably shouldn't have been riding the subway alone to and from school, and to and from visits with my social worker. One day I was riding the subway home after a visit with my social worker, still excited about the new eyeglasses that I worked and saved my own money for, when out of nowhere, a deranged man attacked me. I'd noticed him loudly babbling to himself about some transgression when I got on the train. I didn't pay him any attention though; people are always talking to themselves in the subway. He switched seats several times, and as he did, the train emptied until there were less than a handful of us seated throughout the car. The next thing I knew, he'd cornered me in my seat and commenced to beat me up for several stops.

A white-haired old woman attempted to intervene on my behalf.

"Bitch, mind your own business before I *kick your ass,"* he barked.

She retreated to the far end of the train as he continued to hit me.

The first punch broke my new glasses. All I could do was cover my face and curl up like a baby as this man pounded his fist on my back and head.

As the train pulled into the next station, he suddenly stopped beating me.

I ran from the train and found a police officer standing on the platform. When I quickly explained what happened, he followed me back on the train. The cop handcuffed my attacker and led us into a back room in the subway station.

With the door shut, the police officer took out his Billy club and beat the living daylights out of the man. After administering several hard blows, he paused and asked me if I had seen anything.

"No," I nodded.

And the policeman continued to pummel the guy. As my attacker screamed in pain, the officer kept calling him a punk for picking on a little kid.

I don't know how long the beating lasted or what happened to the deranged man after I left. I just wanted to go home. My face was badly bruised and my body was sore.

◆　　　◆　　　◆

While living with the Eberlys, I decided to try to strengthen my relationship with my grandmother. She had rejected me repeatedly, but I was determined not to abandon the relationship. I started visiting her more frequently, and in the process began developing a relationship with my Uncle Johnny. Everyone was afraid of Uncle Johnny because he had served a long sentence in a facility for the criminally insane. He got excited whenever I came and asked me to read the Bible to him. Almost everyone in the family avoided him except me. I liked him. At the time, he and his sister Cookie were the only people in that family that made me feel I was wanted. I later learned from Grandma that Johnny was my mom's favorite brother.

One day I arrived at my grandmother's house to find a tall man visiting her. Grandma introduced him as her old boyfriend, Vernon. She introduced me as Dee Dee's son.

"Dee Dee's son? Who's Dee Dee?" I wondered to myself.

Seeing the puzzled look on my face, Grandma said, "Sit down, Shane." I figured something big was about to be revealed, and I was right. Grandma told me that Vernon was my birth father's brother.

"Your dad's name is David," she continued. "Dee Dee is a nickname." That's when Vernon spoke up.

"This is Shane? Oh my God! I haven't seen you since you were in diapers!"

The news was shocking, but it felt so good to meet someone who remembered me. I was even more delighted to learn that he knew where my father was. "Would you tell him I'd like to see him," I asked, trying hard to contain my excitement.

"Oh, he wants to see you too."

I couldn't believe it. Someone knew where my father was and he wanted to see me! It was all I could do not to jump up and down screaming. I asked Uncle Vernon to ask my father to get in touch with me right away.

I left Grandma's that day extremely happy. I had decided to stay in touch with her. This one visit alone had given me more hope than I'd had in years that I would finally find one person in this world who really wanted me: my father.

The next day, the phone rang before daylight. It was my father.

"Hello, Shane?"

My heart was racing. "Yes. This is Shane."

"Oh my God!" he screamed. "It's my son!"

His excitement was exhilarating. I could feel how genuinely thrilled he was to find me.

"I have thought about you every day. I love you, son. I've always loved you." He said he had tried to find me but that everyone had lied to him about where I was. They'd even lied to him about my name.

"I thought your name was David," he said. "When can I see you?" "How about today?"

Before I could hang up the phone, my dad was on his way to the Eberlys. I couldn't believe it. As a little boy, I fantasized about meeting my father. I imagined that he was rich and that my being in foster care was just a big mistake. I couldn't wait to see what he was really like.

A few hours later, he arrived.

Right away, I realized he wasn't going to live up to my rich father fantasy. He was driving a loud, rusty, beat-up old car. He didn't even bother to park it. He threw open the door and practically leapt out. We ran to meet one another, and he grabbed me and lifted me off the ground. He held me and kept saying, over and over again, "My son, my son," and he cried.

I was in heaven. I didn't want him to ever let me go. I had never been so happy to see anyone in my life.

"He ain't rich and he ain't tall," I thought. But he is my father. That was enough for me. I searched his face looking for the family resemblance. We looked alike. Finally, after all these years, I looked like somebody else.

When we finally let go of each other, I noticed a very attractive woman stepping from the passenger side of the car.

"This is Joanne," he said proudly.

I was thinking that my dad had really good taste in women, when he asked me if I wanted to ride with them to his apartment.

I immediately said, "Yes."

We piled into the rickety old car and started out for Dad's place in the Fort Apache section of the Bronx. I was so pumped on the drive over I couldn't stop talking. I wanted to tell him everything that had ever happened to me. Who knew if we would ever have this chance again? I listened closely to his every word, too, hoping to find out as much about him and my family as I could. There was no question he was unwilling to answer. We were both so excited. His rusty old car was extremely noisy, so we had to talk loud, and that was okay. I was with my father! I could put up with a little noise. However, what I saw when we pulled up to his place really tested my tolerance.

My father lived in a condemned building. Most of the apartments had been vacated, and wires were running from one apartment to the next to share electricity.

There were plenty of rats and roaches, but no hot water. The ceiling was caving in, and the walls were filthy. However, unbelievably, after a while I didn't care. He was my father, and I wanted to be wherever he was. I told him I was not going back to my foster home, and that I wanted to stay with him.

"This is your home, son; you don't have to go back."

His words made me so happy I was speechless. All I could do was hug him and cry.

I moved in with Dad right away and we started to be better acquainted. I was quite surprised when he told me that I had sixteen brothers and sisters. The woman he married had three children before she died; David Jr., Adrienne, and Debbie were being raised by their maternal grandmother. Another one of the sixteen was in the Caribbean with relatives. The rest were in foster care or adopted. He said they knew about me and that he couldn't wait for me to meet them all.

I had been living with my father for just a few days when it was time for my subway assault case to be heard in court. It felt great having Dad go to court with me. He wanted to see who attacked his son. My chest was poked out so far I almost busted my buttons. "My father will kick your butt if you mess with me," I mouthed to myself as we sat in the courtroom together. I felt protected like never before.

At last, I felt safe, and the outcome of the case was good too. The judge ruled that my attacker had to stay away from me for six months, and victim's compensation paid for the glasses he broke.

Outside the court, my father confronted the man and told him what he'd do to him if he ever saw him again. That small act made my father my hero.

However, just like almost every other good thing in my life, my fantasy of what life would be like with my real family was quickly destroyed. I found out that my father made a living selling stolen toys and bootlegged VHS tapes on the street. He thought I would be a natural at selling things, so took me with him on several occasions. I never really wanted to go. I wanted him to make an honest living. However, I wanted to be with him, and I wanted to make an effort to understand his world.

As days passed, his world kept getting scarier and scarier to me. People came knocking on the door all hours of the night. I was never allowed to answer, and they were never invited in. Once I peeped into his bedroom and saw him scraping a white powder off the folding table beside his bed. I knew enough to know it was cocaine. *Oh my God, my father has cocaine. Is that why people are knocking at the door all night?* As much as I didn't want it to be true, I knew that my dad was distributing and selling drugs.

In spite of his unorthodox enterprises, my dad tried to make living with him as safe and normal as possible. He enrolled me in Alfred E. Smith High School. That meant I had to leave my friends at Julia Richman behind. It was hard to leave because my last few months at Julia Richman were turning out to be some of the best times.

I was finally able to produce the musical play I wrote while living with Reverend Kennedy, "Ebony and the Seven Dudes," the black version of "Snow White and the Seven Dwarfs." Rodney, who was a classmate of mine, introduced me to his mom, and she gave me her typewriter so that I could type my musical. She told me I could keep it, if I promised to take good care of it. I secured backers to finance the costumes and props and found a junior high school that would allow me to use their auditorium; eventually my musical made it to the stage. My father had high hopes that my production would take us from rags to riches. And I thought I was a big dreamer. This was a minor amateur play performed in a junior high school auditorium. It was big fun. I'll always remember it, but it wasn't "Dreamgirls."

During that summer, I signed up for a job as a counselor in a children's day camp. I enjoyed the job, but at the end of each day, I would be exhausted.

The best part of the job was going on field trips with the children. I couldn't believe I was actually being paid to go out and have fun with these kids. On one of our field trips to Jones Beach, a child's beach ball got away. It was already quite a distance from the shore by the time I saw it. Oblivious to any danger, I swam out to retrieve it as the ball traveled even farther out into the Atlantic. Several minutes later, I looked back to the shore and realized how far out into the ocean I was and panicked. I started swimming as hard as I could back to shore, but I tired quickly, and started going under. In a few seconds, I swallowed so much water that I thought I was going to die. A lifeguard saw me, and, after a considerable struggle, managed to pull me safely to shore. Needless to say, I didn't come back with the beach ball, but I did come back with my life. I was so embarrassed afterwards that I wanted to quit that job. With the encouragement of my supervisor and several co-workers, I managed to hang in there and finish the summer.

My father knew I'd made some extra money with the camp counselor job, and he wasn't shy about asking me for it. In fact, he started asking me for money with greater and greater frequency. At first, I didn't mind, but after a while, I noticed that none of it was going to buy groceries. I made the mistake of sharing my frustration with my father's Uncle Erby.

Uncle Erby drank a fifth of Scotch every day, but he had a nice car, nice apartment, and a doting wife, so everybody respected him. I told him that I was the only one in the house working a legitimate job. Uncle Erby said he would talk to Dad. After talking with my father, Uncle Erby reported to me that Dad was *really* pissed. He told Uncle Erby that I was a liar, but Uncle Erby believed me. He gave me money to buy my own food, and invited me to church with him that next Sunday. He suggested that I get involved in the youth fellowship at the church.

"There are some good kids you should get to know at Christ Temple, Shane. I think it will be good for you to meet them."

I agreed to go with Uncle Erby to church the next Sunday. He went out and bought me a new suit and a white cashmere coat for the occasion. When I walked into the church, you couldn't tell me anything—I knew I was looking GOOD! In addition, I really enjoyed the service, too. It was so different from Catholic church. The people were alive and friendly. All the people in the congregation, including his family, were extremely nice to me.

Meanwhile, the situation with my father continued to spiral downward. His idea of good parenting was to give me a joint each morning before I left for school. In addition, the streets in his run-down neighborhood were becoming increasingly dangerous.

One day, I was standing in front of the apartment building when I saw Uncle Bucky, Uncle Erby's son, being chased down the street by several men. They pinned him against a van, took out a gun, put it to his head, and kept firing repeatedly, but the gun didn't go off. I ran upstairs to tell my father, but before Dad could get downstairs with his gun, the men shot Uncle Bucky and took off.

I'd heard that Uncle Bucky was on angel dust and that he was very close to losing his mind. The night before, I had seen him punch a man hard. The man fell to the pavement, hit his head, and later died. In addition, if that wasn't enough trouble, the reason that these men were trying to kill Uncle Bucky was that he told a pregnant woman that he was going to cut her baby out of her body. It was the father of that baby who led the group that attacked and shot Uncle Bucky that night.

When my father and I got to him, Uncle Bucky was on the ground, bleeding badly from his gunshot wound. When the police and ambulance arrived, Uncle Bucky refused to go to the hospital. Afraid for Uncle Bucky's life, my father told the police about the man Uncle Bucky had assaulted the night before. Just as my father planned, Uncle Bucky was taken off the streets and into custody where he would get the medical attention, he needed. Besides, with those men trying to kill him, Dad thought that Uncle Bucky would be safer in jail than on the street. My father believed he had done the right thing. Uncle Erby and Uncle Bucky did not agree.

Nothing I had ever experienced in foster care could compare to what I was now experiencing with my father. I knew that my life would go nowhere fast if I stayed with him. I was certain that, before long, he would have me selling drugs too. The last straw, however, was when I discovered that my father was part of a group that was stealing the identities of dead people in order to fraudulently collect their social security benefits. My father assumed the identity of a James Patton. I can't begin to imagine the crimes he committed in Mr. Patton's name.

I was truly afraid of him now. My father had a gun, he was violent, and he wasn't even using his real name. He often threatened to hit me, but he never did, probably because of my seizures. His first wife had died of a seizure after an argument they had. I think he was afraid to hit me because of what had happened to her. Nevertheless, I was still afraid of him, so I began to plan my departure. If I was going to escape without being caught, I knew I would have to outsmart one extremely nosy neighbor woman. This woman was always perched by her window where she could see, and ultimately report, everything anybody did. I knew that if she saw me moving my things out, she would tell my father. To avoid suspicion, I took just a few things at a time.

That night I hailed a cab, not knowing exactly where I would go. I knew that I couldn't stay with anyone I had introduced my father to because that would make it too easy for him to find me, and I didn't want to put anyone else in danger. Once again, the Moorages came through for me by letting me store my things at their place. When I returned to my father's apartment that evening, he didn't suspect a thing.

My plan was to escape after school the next day. The next morning I got ready for school as usual. My father gave me the customary breakfast joint, said "See ya later, son," and out the door I went.

When the school day ended, it was time to make my getaway, but I didn't know where to go. Confused and scared, I went to Times Square to a place called Covenant House and signed myself in. Looking at the bleak surroundings—all the mattresses on the floor and the kids sleeping on them—I decided that I just couldn't stay there. Instead, I went to the police station across the street in the Port Authority terminal and turned myself in as a runaway from foster care. I shared my story of how I grew up in foster care and that I had recently run away from a group home to go live with my father. I told the officer that I was now running away from my father because I wanted to go back into foster care. I realized running away from foster care was a big mistake, and I wanted another chance.

The officer pulled up their records, but there was no listing of me as a missing person.

"I'll be damned," I thought. The Catholic Home Bureau never even reported me missing from the foster home they had placed me in. "Did they even care that I had run away?" I wondered.

My father was notified and before long, he and his girlfriend showed up at the police station. He told the officer that I was a pathological liar and that the whole story about being in foster care was made up. He swore to them that he had raised me and that I had a history of running away and lying. Obviously, he was very convincing because the police released me into his custody.

Driving back to Dad's place, I was terrified. He threatened me repeatedly.

"If I ever have to come to a police station again to get your ass, you won't live to regret it. Boy, I'll take you out."

At first, I just kept silent, but for some reason I made the mistake of responding to one of his threats.

"Why don't you just go ahead and do it then, just do it!"

Suddenly, he slammed on the brakes, yanked me out, and slammed me against the car.

"What's wrong with you? You want me to whip your ass or something?"

He looked at me, and I just stood there paralyzed. I said not a word for fear he would smack me or worse. Just in time, his girlfriend Joanne jumped out of the car to intervene.

"Shane, don't say anything, just shut up, don't say anything."

She was able to calm my father down and we all got back into the car without anyone getting hurt. As we continued the drive home, I became more determined than ever to get away from him.

The next morning I rushed to school to report my situation to my counselor. At about the same time, my father finally discovered that I had moved some of my things out of his apartment. His girlfriend noticed that most of my clothes were gone, and my father saw that my typewriter was missing, too. He immediately drove to school to find me.

He entered the hallway yelling my name. I could hear him all the way down the hall in the counselor's office where I was hiding. The vice-principal calmed him by threatening to call the police, and after he left the building, my counselor snuck me out the back door and into a taxicab that took me to the Catholic Home Bureau. During the ride, I wondered what I could possibly say to Mr. Pointer. Surely, he wouldn't be as eager to see me again as I would be to see him. Our last meeting hadn't gone particularly well.

I tried to explain everything to Mr. Pointer and told him that I had learned my lesson. I told him that I was horribly afraid of my father.

Then Mr. Pointer looked and me and asked, "What do you want us to do? We're afraid of your father, too." He wanted to know why the Bureau should take me back. Why should they put their lives at risk? "Why should we do this after all you've put us through?"

I had no answer. I just cried and begged them to take me back. However, he was unaffected by my tears. He said he wasn't going to let me manipulate the system anymore and that they weren't going to take me back. By now, I realized I was in big trouble. I had been exposed to life with my father, and I knew it was not the life I wanted to live. I had to think of a way fast to convince the Catholic Home Bureau to take me back or else.

Finally, it dawned on me to remind Mr. Pointer I was still a ward of the state and that he and the agency were responsible for me until I was 18 years old. "I'm not leaving until you find me a home," I declared!

6

THE STORM IS OVER

o o o o o o o o o o o o o o o o o o o o o o o o o o o o o o o o o o
I've been racing for years and still no finish line…then
somehow, my beginning stepped right in
and then, faith became my friend.
I hollered help because I was lost and then I felt a strong wind,
and a small voice saying the storm is over.
R. Kelly

My ultimatum worked. Mr. Pointer agreed to take me back into foster care. That same day, he found a place for me in the Rego Park group home in Queens.

I started attending Christ Temple, Uncle Derby's church, every Sunday. The pastor's family would often pick me up and bring me back to the group home, since they lived in Queens too. On the way home from church one Sunday, something happened that I can only describe as a miracle. A wintry mix of snow and sleet was falling one night when the pastor was driving his wife, his two daughters, and me from church back to Queens. As we were crossing the Queensboro Bridge, the car started sliding and spinning out of control. Given the usually heavy traffic on the bridge and the severity of the spin, we were almost certain to be hit by a car or careen down a steep embankment. I just knew we were going to die. The pastor tried desperately to get control of the car, but with no success. We were still sliding and spinning from one side of the bridge to the other when the pastor's wife said, "In the Name of Jesus." The moment she spoke those words the car came to a complete stop, facing the embankment and clear of oncoming traffic. It was nothing short of a miracle. Only God could have enabled me to survive this and so many other life-threatening situations. That incident went a long way toward reinforcing my faith in God.

That brush with death caused me to take a closer look at my life and take stock of where I was and where I was going. I was 16 years old and only had two years left as a ward of the state. Confronting the reality of my situation, I decided it was time to get it together. I had finally come to realize that I could not allow the pain and trouble I was experiencing to prevent me from achieving great things. It was time to move past the troubles in my life and focus on the opportunities that lay ahead. I needed to get myself ready for life after foster care, I had to get serious about my education, and I had to start planning a successful future.

Once I was settled into my new group home, I started taking advantage of every opportunity afforded me. No one was going to do anything to deter me from reaching my goal of graduating. In addition to my regular classes, I took independent studies and did all different kinds of things to make up the classes I had missed from moving around so much. I took double loads so that I could graduate on time. With every success, my self-confidence grew. My success did have a down side, however. Sometimes I got into fights because there were some residents of the group home who would call me names like church boy and punk because I appeared to be smart and goal oriented.

Since I didn't have family to visit on weekends like most of the other teens in the group home, I would sometimes spend weekends with my "big brother" Joe. It was always a treat whenever he would pick me up in that sharp navy-blue

Chrysler New Yorker, and allow me to get away from the group home for a while. Sometimes, while I was away on weekend visits or at church, the other kids would break into my room and steal things. Otherwise, my time away from the home was enjoyable and very positive.

In spite of the conflicts, I did manage to make some good friends while I was at Rego Park who seemed to be as motivated as I was to turn their lives around. One of my friends was Kenny who, having grown up in an established white family, was sure that being in a group home with nothing but black and Latino kids was nothing more than a bad dream. He was determined to get out of there as quickly as possible and never look back. To make things easier on him, I agreed to become his roommate. He often referred to me as the only sane one in the group-home.

In my homeroom, class was a very attractive young lady, Tara. She was very slim with long, soft, bouncy hair. I was always a fool for a woman with pretty hair. We didn't connect right away, but that was okay because I really wanted to hook up with the most popular girl in the school, Tracy. As luck would have it, Tracy asked me out and I jumped at the opportunity. We hit it off right away, and things were going great. Then suddenly one day Tracy became as cold as ice towards me. When I asked her what was up, I could hardly believe her response. "I just wanted to prove to the girls that I could get you if I wanted to," she boasted. "Mission accomplished." I had no idea girls did that kind of stuff. She had no idea she had broken my heart. I am pleased to say, however, that it was only broken for about a week. That's how long it took me to recover and start making moves towards Tara. She lived in a group home that was walking distance from mine, so one day we walked home together. We liked each other from the start. We started sneaking in and out of each other's group homes just to be together. Before long, she became my high school sweetheart.

While at the Rego Park group home, I was enrolled in my fifth high school, John Bowne. When the school administrators looked at my credits and absenteeism rate, they predicted that I wouldn't graduate on time. That was very discouraging because I didn't want to be in the group home one day longer than I had to, and I wanted my high school diploma as soon as possible. Things started looking up; however, when I learned about Satellite Academy High, a unique school where I could complete independent study assignments that would help me make up the required credits for graduation. The school's principal assured me that I could do a lot of catching up, but he couldn't promise me that I would be able to graduate on time. But I refused to be discouraged. In fact, I looked forward to the challenge. In addition to independent course work, I participated in the cooperative work-study program. This enabled me to put money in my pocket and gave me the chance to work for the Federal Aviation Administration (FAA) in the Noise Abatement Office. That job helped me develop a strong work ethic and gave me another opportunity to chart my own destiny. I couldn't say enough good things about Satellite Academy High. I told my roommate KB how great this school was and that I was very likely to make up my credits and graduate on time. After hearing me talk with such enthusiasm, KB enrolled as well.

In school, I discovered that I had the ability to lead and motivate people. I ran for president of the student government and won. Out of frustration with the quality of food and supervision at the group home, I created a newsletter called the Rego Park Post. I encouraged the other kids to submit poems or otherwise express their frustrations or observations. I typed the newsletter on my old typewriter and circulated it throughout the group home and to the foster care agency. To our amazement, the agency started listening and making the changes, we wanted. We got results by channeling our energy productively. It was amazing.

As the year progressed, it finally became clear that I would graduate on time. I was so relieved. I made it! In spite of it all, I made it. At the senior awards assembly, I was stunned when they announced that I was the valedictorian of my class. Could I possibly be the smartest person in the school? How did this happen? I wasn't as competitive about grades as other students were. The guy who just wanted to graduate on time was graduating with honors, and I accepted the accolades with pride and dignity as Tara looked on. After attending six different high schools, three within my junior and senior years alone, I was graduating valedictorian. The New York School of Printing, Julia Richman for the Performing Arts, St. Thomas Aquinas, Alfred E. Smith, and John Bowne were fragments of my high school experience, but Satellite Academy was the one where I earned my diploma and the graduating class's highest honor.

Tara and I went to the senior prom together. I wore a white tuxedo with tails. Tara was positively stunning in a lilac custom-designed satin gown and hat. We arrived in a white limousine, and when we walked in as the Prom King and Queen, everyone stopped and applauded. I felt as if I had been transformed from a frog into a prince.

A whole new world was opening up for me, and the next step on my journey was college. I really needed some guidance on that subject, so I spoke with Dr. Lewis, my psychologist. Dr. Lewis suggested that I pick a small college because she thought I might find a large university overwhelming. I followed her advice, and every college I applied to accepted me. I couldn't believe so many doors were busting wide open.

I called Mom Jamison to give her the good news and she could hardly believe I was graduating, let alone as valedictorian. She agreed to come to the ceremony in part, I suspect, because she thought I was lying and she was going to have to see it for herself.

I called my grandmother to tell her about graduation and being named valedictorian. She was so proud of me. I asked her if she would be willing to give me a special graduation gift: the telephone number of my great-grandmother, Flossy. I knew I was asking a lot because Grandma and her mom Flossy did not get along at all. But it was important to me to try to have a relationship with my great-grandmother, and I wanted to invite her to my graduation. I was very grateful to Grandma for putting aside her differences long enough to give me the number. I called my great-grandmother right away, and Tara and I went to visit her.

My great-grandmother lived on the Upper West Side in Harlem. She had a beautiful apartment with French imported furniture and a player baby grand piano. "Now I know where I get my taste. It must have skipped two generations or something," I joked. We all had a good laugh. Then my great-grandmother began to talk about my mom, Sherry. Great-Grandma told me that she thought that Sherry's life would have turned out different if she had been allowed to raise her. Great-Grandma wanted very much to raise Sherry, but Grandma wouldn't let her. I wondered if that was why Great-Grandma Flossy and Grandma had been estranged all these years. I wondered if things would have been different for Sherry. Would I even be here? I guess I'll never know.

Tara and I enjoyed our visit, and I was very happy to have established a relationship with my great-grandmother. However, there was still at least one more family rift I wanted to mend. I wanted to be reunited with my brother KB, and I asked my new social worker Ray to help me. Ray wasn't sure he could help me get back together with KB, but he was able to update me on what KB had been up to since I'd last seen him. I was saddened to learn that KB's adoption by Rev. Kennedy fell through. After that, he went to Hillside Children's Center for a year and a half. Another couple, a Mr. and Mrs. Myers, took an interest in him, and eventually adopted KB. After the adoption, Mr. and Mrs. Myers got a stern warning from Rev. Kennedy that I was a bad influence, and that they had better keep KB away from me.

I asked my social worker to ask the Myers if they would let me send a cassette tape that they could screen. Ray gave it a shot, and The Myers agreed. After screening the tape, Mr. and Mrs. Myers concluded that I was anything but a bad influence. In fact, they thought seeing me might help. KB was acting out. They decided to send him to New York City from Rochester, New York, to attend my graduation and to give us a chance to reconnect.

Graduation day finally came, and I was reunited with my brother KB. "It's good to see you, big brother," he said, as we embraced one another. "I'm so proud of you." It didn't matter what anyone else said or didn't say after that. As I looked out on the audience when I delivered my valedictorian's speech—seeing my grandmother in the audience, along with Great Grandma, Mrs. Jamison and KB—I saw the fibers of my life coming back together. My grandmother started bragging about how proud she was until my great-grandmother told her, "Be quiet, the only one deserving of any credit for that boy is his mother, Mrs. Jamison." I agreed with great-grandmother on principle, but this really was something for us all to celebrate. As a family, this was our celebration, regardless of the history and all of its pain. It seems the celebration had barely started when it was time for KB to go back to Rochester. I promised to stay in touch and that I would visit him. In fact, I decided to attend Elmira College, which was only a couple of hours away from Rochester, just to be closer to him.

Immediately after high school graduation, I worked three jobs at the same time to earn money for school. I was a file clerk at the Social Security Administration on the weekdays, a front desk clerk at Best Western Hotel weeknights, and I worked at the nightclub Justine's on weekends. Later that summer, I found out Tara was pregnant. I begged her to keep our baby, but she wouldn't. Even her group home director advised Tara to have an abortion. In fact, she tried to discourage me from pursuing a romantic relationship with Tara. "You will eventually outgrow her, Shane," she predicted. I couldn't believe that a nun was saying this and that she was encouraging Tara to have an abortion. I told Tara that I was willing to forgo Elmira College and attend Hunter College, which was closer to her, so she, our baby, and I could be a family. I thought I had her convinced to keep the baby. But while I was working at the hotel one night, she called to inform me that she was on her way to have an abortion, and that there was nothing I could do to change her mind. That night, I vowed never to have anything to do with Tara again.

The day finally came when I would leave the Rego Park group home and become a freshman at Elmira College in upstate New York. I was determined to major in anything but social work, and I ultimately decided on health and human services. Maybe subconsciously I made the decision to be a health care major because Ma Jamison had gone back to school to become a registered nurse.

Things went great that first semester. New York State covered my room and board, and my tuition was covered through Pell Grants, student loans, and a partial scholarship from Elmira. I was enjoying myself and doing well in classes. But as I was preparing to go home for the Christmas break, I realized something: I had no home to go back to. All my college friends were making plans to go home and spend time with their families. Meanwhile the group home had given away my room to a new resident. They did however offer me the option of sleeping on their couch. The situation was a painful reminder that abused and neglected children who overcome tremendous challenges and manage, against all odds, to survive the foster care system, end up with no place to go home to. It didn't seem right for them, and it certainly didn't feel right for me. There was, I concluded, something very wrong with the system.

I had no family to turn to the night I was returning from New York City from a semester break and my car broke down in the mountains of upstate New York. I couldn't phone home. There was no one to call for help. I had no family. I was fortunate enough to get help from a stranger who put me up for the night, paid for my busted tire, and sent me on my way the next morning. I shudder to think what could have happened if I hadn't been so lucky.

It was a great comfort when the Myers, my brother KB's adoptive family, invited me to be a part of their family. They would send me care packages at school and give me a place to stay during holidays. I didn't bother to explain to my classmates that I had been a foster child. I just claimed Mom and Dad Myers as my parents too. It felt good to say that my dad is an Associate Professor at SUNY Brockport and that my mom is the Minority Business Enterprise Officer for the City of Rochester. In fact, Dad Myers was brave and patient enough to teach me how to drive during that second year when I started coming to Rochester more frequently on breaks.

College life continued to go well. I stayed at Elmira College for the first two years. Then I applied to Morehouse College and was accepted. But suddenly, a bit of unexpected news was threatening to derail my train. It seems that Tara's visit to Elmira a few months earlier had resulted in another pregnancy. She was three months pregnant, and this time I was determined that she wasn't going to have an abortion. The situation was further complicated by the fact that things were supposedly over between Tara and me, and I had started dating and fallen madly in love with Janice, a fellow Elmira student. Janice was not only one of the prettiest young ladies on campus; she was one of the smartest too. But my relationship with Janice was in danger now that Tara had announced her pregnancy. Janice's first reaction to the pregnancy news was that we would survive it. She understood my foster care history and knew how much I'd want to be there for my kid. But being a dad from a distance was not acceptable for me. So I told Janice that we had to end it so that I could give Tara and me a chance for the baby's sake. Janice said she understood, and we said our good-byes.

If getting pregnant was, Tara's way of getting us back together, it worked. Because of her and the baby, I decided not to go to Morehouse. My big brother Joe was outraged. He told me that I'd be throwing my life away if I didn't insist that Tara abort the baby. I didn't agree. I could not sanction an abortion of my child because every time I look in the mirror, I am reminded of how close my mother came to aborting me and I can't help but feel the presence of God's intervention on my behalf. Instead, I enlisted in the Navy's BOOST Program, a preparatory program for commission status. This was my way of ensuring that our baby would not have to go through the things I went through. Joining the service put me in a position to provide for both of them. What better way, I figured, to complete my education while being able to support my child.

I was scheduled to leave for the Navy's BOOST program on June 28, and the baby was due between June 28 and July 5. Although I wanted to be around for the delivery, in my mind, securing a future for the family was more important. However, Tara disagreed and insisted that I be there for the delivery. I met with my recruiter and forfeited my slot in BOOST, which, unfortunately, meant forgoing the opportunity for commission. After I received my associate's degree on June 5 from Elmira College, Tara and I departed for New York City.

My old Volkswagen had worn-out shock absorbers, and I guess the bumpy ride back to New York might have caused Tara to go into labor on June 7, three to four weeks before she was due. Tiffany Monique Salter was born at about 12:30 am on June 8. Tiffany was born crying and shivering, but when the nurse placed her in my arms, the shivering and crying stopped. As a tear fell from my eye, I looked into hers and promised that she would never know the kind of pain I had known. Everything I did from that day forward was for my precious baby girl. After Tiffany was born, Tara went to live in a teen mom and baby program. Before I left for the Navy, we were secretly married. I wanted to be sure that Tiffany never felt illegitimate if I lost my life in the Navy.

My departure date for the Navy was now September 23. Meanwhile, I quickly found the best-paying job I could find in New York City, which at the time was in the housekeeping department of a Jewish nursing home. As a union member, I was actually making more money mopping, waxing, and buffing floors than many of the administrative staffers were making. I wore a gray housekeeping uniform, which I found humbling given that I had just graduated college. I found people in the building usually didn't want to speak to me just because I wore that uniform. When those administrative staffers turned their noses up at me, I would mumble under my breath, "I probably make more money than you anyway." Because of the terrible way I was treated, I made a promise to myself that I would never look down on anybody because of his or her job.

I worked as many hours as they would give me, just to be sure that Tiffany and Tara were well taken care of. When September 23 came, I left for boot camp in San Diego, California as planned.

Just a few weeks into boot camp, Tara wrote me a" Dear John" letter. There I was getting my butt whipped in the blazing heat, and I get a letter from her saying "I'm tired of you being away, if this is the way our life is going to be, then I want a divorce." What was I to do? I didn't want to be in boot camp—I was only there because I had a family that needed instant income security. It was our ticket out of foster care for certain, I thought. How could she send me that kind of letter? Damn, how dare she. Here I go again, I thought. Not in my adult life, too. Right out the gate, trying to create my own family and she's ready to walk out on me just like everyone else. I just wanted to throw in the towel right there and say forget it, what's this fight really for? How much more of this will I have to put up with? Does anyone hang in there with you for the long haul? I almost started feeling sorry for myself. Then I looked at a picture of Tiffany and suddenly everything was all right. It was all about Tiffany, my baby girl, I reminded myself. That is what the fight is all about; she will not have to pay for the sins of her parents the rest of her life.

I wrote back to Tara and told her not to ever send me a letter like that again. I reminded her that I was getting my ass kicked in boot camp for her and Tiffany and didn't need that kind of distraction. Later I learned that the Dear John letter was Tara's way of letting me know she was having an affair. I believe that affair resulted in her third pregnancy, even though she claimed I was the father. Apparently Tara found out she was pregnant again a few weeks after I left for boot camp, and, for a second time, she had an abortion.

I was determined to complete boot camp and become a Hospital Corpsman. That would enable me to provide for my family and ultimately become a Hospital Administrator. To reach that goal, I had to re-enroll in college immediately after boot camp. I could see myself running a clinic, a department within a medical facility or maybe even serving as the CEO of a hospital somewhere. I had big dreams, and I had a plan. But that plan was seriously threatened when I couldn't pass my swim test. After failing for the fourth time, I wrote Tara and said, "I may not make it. They are threatening to kick me out if I don't pass the next time. If they do, I guess I'll try the Air Force," I wrote. Thank God, I passed the next time and my Navy career was back on track.

I was proud when I graduated from high school as valedictorian, but that was nothing compared to the pride I felt when I graduated from boot camp. As we marched and they played the National Anthem, I got chills up my spine. I had officially become one of America's own. I finally belonged somewhere. I had an identity as a sailor in the United States Navy. After graduating, I remained in San Diego for the rest of the year where I completed requirements to become a Hospital Corpsman. I was asked to list the top three places I wanted to be stationed. My first choice was Charleston, South Carolina, because I heard it was a big Navy Town, which would be a lot of fun, and because it wasn't too far from Tara's mother in Hilton Head. My second choice was National Naval Medical Center in Bethesda, Maryland because I was told that's where the "big brass" were, and that if I was noticed there, it could really propel my career. I ended up in Bethesda, and while stationed there, I completed my rotation on the inpatient wards, working deadly rotating shifts. I did so well that in record time I petitioned to be assigned to a clinic so that I could go back to school. My petition was honored and I was then assigned for the next few years to the Pediatric Acute Care Clinic. I enrolled in the base's external degree program through Southern Illinois University at Carbondale, majoring in health care management. Eventually, I became the Senior Corpsman in the clinic and my superiors strongly encouraged me to enroll in the Armed Forces Medical School to become a physician. My commander, who was impressed with my ambition and clinical skills, said if I wanted it, he would make it happen.

Well, I knew I did not want to be a physician bad enough to endure all that I would have to do to get there. Secondly, I knew that the support I had at home from Tara was weak at best. Tara resented the amount of time I spent on my studies. We were about twenty years old and Tara felt we should be clubbing more and having an active social life. I promised her that would come in time, and I tried to convince her that my education was an investment in our future. However, she obviously was not very committed to our marriage. Shortly after being assigned to the pediatric clinic and relocating her and Tiffany from New York, I found an un-mailed love letter she had written to another man. As much as I wanted to create my own family, my ego could not handle the affair and I asked for a divorce. It was ugly. We fought and fought a long time before agreeing to go our separate ways.

Initially, we agreed that I would have custody of Tiffany. Then Tara suddenly changed her mind, and I was devastated. She figured she could get money from me if she took Tiffany with her. To further complicate our impending separation, Tara was pregnant again. Despite my objections to the contrary, Tara decided to have another abortion. "I'll have a better chance of finding someone with one child than with two," she said. At that point, for the first time, I think I actually wanted her to have an abortion. I even gave her the money for it. I was, however, quite devastated to learn later that we had aborted twins.

The day Tara left with my baby girl my world shattered. I refused to fight for custody because I didn't want to establish a precedent for her using Tiffany as a way to get at me. To add salt to the wound, Tara decided that they were moving to Hilton Head, South Carolina to live with Tara's mother. She knew how much I loved Tiffany. Why would she move so far away? Why wouldn't she just go back to New York, which I could get to in four hours? Now, the one person that mattered most to me, Tiffany, was being taken away. Shortly after Tara left, I moved into a town house with two roommates.

One weekend I planned a drive to New York to visit Joe and show him my new car. I called a couple of nights prior, to confirm that I was still coming, but got no answer. I found that odd because as a senior employee at Western Electric he had instant access to the latest technological equipment. Surely, he had at least an answering machine. After not being able to get in touch with him, I decided to postpone the trip until I could be sure Joe was in town. The next Tuesday, the Red Cross summoned me.

When I arrived at the Red Cross offices, they told me that Joe had been robbed and killed in New York. Now I had another reason to hate New York. My head was still spinning as I learned that Joe was going to be buried the next day. I took the first flight available, but, unfortunately, it was delayed, and I missed the funeral. A friend picked me up at the airport and rushed me to the cemetery. Joe's casket had already been laid in the ground. I never have to see him or say good-bye. The pain was even deeper than when I learned of my mother's death. I was devastated. My big brother, mentor, friend and confidant was gone. I made my way to where the family had gathered after Joe's funeral. I spoke with a friend of Joe's who told me that I should never try to find a replacement for Joe in my life because there would never be one. That was the best advice he could have given me. No one understood me like Joe, no one motivated me like Joe, and no one loved me like Joe. Every day of my life, I still miss him. He was my hero. I wish he could see the man I've become. He'd be pleased to know I hung in there in spite of it all.

A year later, my ex-wife called and said that she could no longer provide for Tiffany and asked me to take permanent custody. What was I supposed to do? I was living with two other guys in a three-bedroom town house in Silver Spring, Maryland. But I couldn't let that stand in the way. Somehow, I worked it out with Zarick and Jesse to have Tiffany come live with us for a while. Tiffany and I would share the same room at first, but shortly after she arrived, Zarick moved out, and Tiffany picked up her own room.

Tiffany was two years old when I got custody of her. Even as a single parent, I was determined that she would have a life that was befitting of a princess. She went with me everywhere. Eventually, Tiffany and I were able to get our own place in Rockville, Maryland. In order to finish my degree and earn additional income, I had girlfriends watching Tiffany in shifts. I was enrolled in school full-time, working part-time, and fulfilling my last year in the Navy.

I completed my four years in the Navy, but I didn't reenlist. On the day of my discharge, I stood in front of the National Naval Medical Center with Tiffany beside me. "Here in Maryland is where we will plant our roots," I vowed. "We will redefine what it means to be a Salter."

I decided that I would transition from Navy active duty to Air Force Reserve. Now to many people that didn't seem to make much sense, given that, the Navy and the Air Force are not at all similar, but that made it all the more exciting for me. I was always intrigued by the Air Force. I was offered a position as an entry-level supervisor at Children's Hospital in Washington, DC, and I joined the Air Force Reserve. I must say, though, the Air Force experience only confirmed how much more I liked the Navy. I privately questioned the logic of my decision to join the Air Force until I met this sweet unassuming young lady. She had a radiant smile, and never was a strand of hair out of place. And as far as substance goes, she was the most solid woman I'd met. She was different from any other woman in the reserve unit. However, at first I wasn't interested in her romantically. I didn't think she was my type, but I certainly wanted her to be my friend.

After promising month after month to call her, I ran into her and struck up a conversation about a challenge I was facing. Tiffany was about to be christened the sleeves on her beautiful white christening dress were too long, and I didn't know how to sew. Gloria agreed to take the dress home and alter it for me. After the christening, I invited her over for dinner with Tiffany and me as a gesture of gratitude. That was the night I discovered that Gloria was adopted. Even though her adoption experience was considerably different from mine, somehow I felt she might be able to identify with me on some level.

7

LOVE DADDY

o o o o o o o o o o o o o o o o o o o o o o o o o o o o o o o o o o o

my children, I wish these things for you…
a family that has a special place
for each one's gentle face
parents that lift your self-esteem
while nurturing the potential of your dreams
love that comes from me to you
these things I wish your whole life through.

you see my children when I was small
I didn't feel much love at all
I grew up in so much pain
while other children scorned my name
and all of the adults that were suppose to protect me
never stayed, never kept me

so here's my chance to give to you
those precious things I wanted too
they are the things I whole so dear
a family built with love, a love that's sincere.

one day you'll understand my pain
but more importantly, the love I gave
I know you'll love your children too the way your daddy has loved you
remember the things I never knew
until the day, God gave me you.

Love Daddy
S. Salter

Gloria and I became good friends at first, and then one day I realized that I was romantically attracted to her. I realized something had changed for me when she tried to hook me up with a friend of hers who was not even in the same league as Gloria. Right after that set-up, I expressed my interest in Gloria, and we started dating. I was having a real hard time getting up the nerve for that first kiss. Then my friend Harold told me, you had better kiss that woman before she thinks something is wrong with you. Well, the pressure was on. We were standing by the car saying good-bye, after a date one night, while Tiffany waited in the back seat; when I finally kissed Gloria, Tiffany was so excited she called her Mommy. That's when Gloria did something that truly impressed me. She said to Tiffany, "I'm not your mother, sweetie," and gave her a hug. She took an awkward situation and handled it directly, yet with great sensitivity.

After that first kiss, I knew I wanted to marry Gloria, but I hadn't filed for divorce from Tara. I had told Tara if she wanted a divorce, she was going to pay for it. I didn't have much money, and what I did have was for Tiffany. I told her to just file and I wouldn't contest it. After taking such a stance, I knew if I sent her divorce papers, she would know something was up and become obstructive just for the hell of it. Gloria made it clear to me that I shouldn't even think about proposing to her until my divorce was final. Well, under the circumstances, I thought I might have to wait for years. Then a few weeks later, a miracle happened. Unsolicited, divorce papers arrived from an attorney in South Carolina who was representing Tara. I took it as a sign. Gloria is the woman for me and she's the stepmother Tiffany deserves. Right away, I started preparing to purchase a ring, and again, Gloria dropped a gentle hint.

"If you need help paying for It, let me know." I interpreted that as code for "Don't bring me no diamond chip, nothing less than a half karat will do."

I couldn't stop laughing, but I also got the message. I found a great ring, I proposed, and Gloria accepted.

Meanwhile, my little brother, KB, had been living with me for almost a year. KB's said his plan was to go into the service, but I don't think those were ever his true intentions. I leveraged my reputation and relationships to get him a job at Children's Hospital only to see him terminated within the first month. Fortunately, not many people knew he was my brother, and the embarrassment was minimal.

KB would take every opportunity to remind me of the pain he endured when I left him behind in Rochester.

"Enough already," I remember saying. "How many times are we going to talk about this?" I tried repeatedly to explain that I made the best decision I could under the circumstances. "For crying out loud, I was 15." I shouted. This underlying issue remains unresolved for him. Every other conversation. between the two of us, circles back to when he was 12 years old in Rochester.

The tension between us escalated to a fistfight in my apartment once. A few inches taller than me, he thought he could whip me, but I was equally determined to show him otherwise. It should never get to that given the history of this relationship. Our rage was real and intense never the less. I was afraid that future fights might lead to the death of one of us. Therefore, I could not continue to expose Tiffany, who was now five years old, to that nonsense and I asked him to leave.

KB moved to Washington, DC, angry with me, and very uncertain about where he belonged. He resolved to survive by any means necessary. I would hear from him from time to time, but our relationship had become increasingly strained. It was challenging, but we never lost sight of the fact that we were brothers and loved each other very much. Therefore, when KB called in need of a place to stay, I offered my apartment. It was getting close to my wedding day, so Tiffany and I were spending most of our time at Gloria's anyway. I gave KB my apartment, fully furnished, with the understanding that he would pay the utilities. KB was elated and I was glad that I could do something to help him, but it turned out to be a big mistake. I went by the apartment one day to pack some of my things, and was shocked to find the apartment filthy. The electricity hadn't been paid, the lights didn't work and the refrigerator was completely defrosted. If that wasn't enough, I walked into Tiffany's room to find her ceramic piggy bank shattered into a million pieces, and all of the money we had been saving since her birth was gone. My heart was shattered into a million pieces too. He couldn't have hurt me more if he tried.

For weeks, I couldn't find KB, but he resurfaced just before the wedding. Originally, he was supposed to be a groomsman, but I did not want to rely on him for a role that wasn't easily replaceable, so I asked him to perform the less demanding task of escorting distinguished guests down the aisle. He was supportive and agreed. Meanwhile, Gloria and I had already started house shopping. We found a beautiful home in Fort Washington, Maryland, on almost two acres of land, and we were able to move in a few months before the wedding.

The day arrived for me to marry my best friend. Ebenezer A.M.E. church in Fort Washington, Maryland was beautifully decorated for the occasion. KB escorted Gloria's adoptive mother down the aisle. Despite several knee surgeries and having to use a walker, she was determined to make that walk. I was represented by three sets of parents: Mom and Dad Myers, Mom and Dad Moorages, and Mom Jamison. Pop Jamison wasn't able to make it, but the Jamison's son Robbie was there. Was I glad to see my foster brother? My grandmother was there, beaming with pride along with my mother's baby brother, Uncle Pierre. My mom's sister Jewell, who was now the latest family casualty of drug addiction, used the occasion to create a scene. She insisted that she should have a rose and be escorted to her seat as an honored guest. I'm sure the entire church could hear her yelling in the vestibule "She was my dead mother's sister and should be given her props."

She refused to be quiet until one of the hosts took the rose off her garment and gave it to my aunt. Then KB escorted her down the aisle.

With all the drama behind us, I was finally, after so many years, about to have the family I had always dreamed of. Attired in his dress Air Force blues, Technical Sergeant Douglass Bell almost stole the show rolling out the red carpet in cadence. The sight of my sister Shanique as a junior bridesmaid and Tiffany as the flower girl brought tears to my eyes. However, nothing could compare to how radiant Gloria was. For the first time, nothing about my past mattered because our future was so bright. I was on my way to building the family for Tiffany and me that was always in my dreams.

A year later, our first child together, Brittney Nicole was born. Gloria and I learned in advance that we were having a girl, and while I tried to be certain not to let it show, this time I was really hoping for a boy. After sixteen hours of labor, the baby's heart rate was dropping and the doctor decided to perform an emergency cesarean section. When Brittney emerged, she was blue and not breathing. At that moment, I thought I was being punished for wanting a boy instead of just being thankful for a healthy baby. I prayed to God in that minute to save our baby and spare my wife.

"She doesn't deserve this. Please save our baby," I pleaded. Within minutes, Brittney was breathing.

After our second daughter, Courtney Shanade, was born a few years later, we realized that if we were going to have sons, they would have to be adopted.

Our first son, Rico Giovanni, came to us at the age of six. Rico was bi-racial, too dark for white families and considered undesirable by most black families. The combination of his race, his age, and his mother's history of schizophrenia, classified him as hard to place. However, he was anything but undesirable to Gloria and me. We couldn't wait to meet him.

Our first meeting was so exciting, and I couldn't get over the fact that he looked so much like me. The agency told me that although he had been diagnosed with separation anxiety as a preschooler, he had responded well to treatment and was a well-adjusted kid. He was wearing checkered pants and a striped shirt with a coat full of dirt and grease. We wondered what kind of foster home sends a child to meet prospective parents dressed like that. I gathered a strategic one: to make the prospective parents feel overwhelmed with sympathy to move quickly and get him out of there. Gloria and I instantly decided that he would join our family.

During his first pre-placement weekend visit with us, Rico's responses to questions seemed programmed. For example, if I asked him why he was doing something he shouldn't have been doing, his response was "because I'm bad." It became clear that these obviously programmed responses were meaningless to him. I also noticed that he sometimes struggled to understand questions. I wondered if he was hard of hearing.

Gloria and I met with Rico's teachers, hoping they could shed some light on his behavior. The teacher we spoke to showed us Rico's consistent A and B course work. She knew him well, and was certain that all he needed was to be adopted. "Please give him a home. He is so sweet; he just needs a good home," she said.

My heart ached for him, just as my heart ached when I was in Rico's shoes as a little boy hoping that someone would give me a home. They brought him into the classroom that day dressed in purple corduroy pants that seemed to be about two sizes too small. All I could think about was getting him some new clothes and trashing those tight purple pants. He must have been humiliated in the Washington, DC public school dressed like that. Later that day we met his foster parents, and I was reminded of when I was a foster child with the Bradfords. Just like the Bradfords, Rico's foster mother did not intend to adopt him, but they had adopted a little girl that came into their home after Rico. The original plan to reunite Rico with his birth father didn't work out. This cleared the way for us to become his family.

Rico made it clear that he didn't like his name and wanted to be named after me. I couldn't have been prouder, and I could certainly understand how he could associate belonging and security with his name. However, I told him that one of the few things he would receive from his birth mother was his name, and that I thought he should keep part of it. Therefore, he became Shane Lenard Rico Salter, and I added Rico to my name to become Shane Lenard Rico Salter, Sr.

Shortly after he came to us, I noticed he was having difficulties in school. At first, I figured the problems had arisen because he was still adjusting to life with us. However, when things didn't seem to get any better, I made an appointment with the Department of Psychiatry and Speech Pathology at Children's Hospital where I worked as hospital administrator. The psychologist gave us several diagnoses, but his major problem was receptive language disorder, which is similar to dyslexia. Gloria and I addressed his needs through special education services and in home therapy. The following year, Shane Rico's adoption became final.

From the start, we went to great lengths to reassure Shane Rico that his family was permanent and that we were never going to give up on him. The more we reassured him, the more comfortable he became in displaying his anger. Thanks to Shane Rico, we had too many busted walls and windows to count over the years. I found it interesting that Shane Rico would do most of his damage when I wasn't in the house. Tiffany would always say, "Dad, he acts very different when you're not home."

I rather naively tried to write it off as normal behavior for a little boy. I believed that he behaved differently around me because he felt that I was the only one who understood him. I'd been in his shoes before, and I did everything I could to let him know he was unconditionally accepted by me. He was such a likable kid; there was no reason for him not to fit in. However, he didn't. For his own reasons, he was drawn to me and always wanted to be around his dad.

I began to notice Shane Rico didn't enjoy the things other children his age enjoyed. He relished the basic things. On one occasion, we were crossing a bridge while riding in the car and his reaction caught me by surprise as he jumped with excitement at the beauty and magnitude of the open body of water. He just took it all in and enjoyed the moment.

Shane Rico and I looked forward to our special moments in the car. He would ask me questions about everything and we'd sing our favorite song *"All by myself...don't want to be...all by myself any more..."* whenever it played on the cassette tape. We would sing it on the way to the store, on the way to school, and even when we went fishing. We always sang. He would crack up watching me in animation acting out some of the lyrics to other songs every now and then. Each time I'd say, "Hold on, that's my favorite song." until one day, Shane Rico busted me out and said, "Dad, they're all your favorite songs." I guess he was right. I love music and so does he.

Shane Rico had been in foster care since he was one year old. His father was an alcoholic. His mother suffered from schizophrenia. We were told that he was predisposed but we didn't know that sons of moms were at higher risk. We thought it was possible not probable. Truthfully, I don't think it would have made a difference in our decision. However, we never watched for it or thought about it again. He was a challenging child from the beginning, but he was my first son, so I just thought he was different from the girls because he had more testosterone. However, the holes in the walls at the house were getting larger with each new outburst. Shane Rico was having more than just a little trouble handling his anger, I started to realize. The tantrums grew more frequent. Shane Rico started getting angry at things that didn't make sense, like if somebody just looked at him wrong. The other children in the family started warning me. They would say, "You should see the way he looks at mom sometimes when you're gone; he looks at her like he's gonna snap when she tells him to do something."

I thought back to my anger and rage when I was a kid but couldn't identify with this. His behavior seemed extreme at times; especially the day he was confronted about something he did and reacted by flying off to his room putting his fist through the window. Now, let's keep it real, I almost kicked his you know what.

"Have you lost your mind?" I asked.

Shortly afterwards he was hospitalized for depression. He was flat, and not responding to anything. He didn't want to play and he didn't get excited about anything. My concerns grew deeper when one night Gloria did a bed check and didn't find him. After searching the house, she located him playing with candles. He had put all of our lives in jeopardy. Desperate times call for desperate measures. We both looked at each other and declared we needed help. We called a meeting at school and got him a new Individualized Educational Plan (IEP), which called for intensive psychological support services in the classroom along with a smaller class size. Through Prince George's County, we were also afforded in-home counseling as well, but not much progress was made.

Months later, Grandma agreed to come down from New York to watch the children so Gloria and I could take a trip together. The two of us hadn't had a break together in years. Finding someone to watch the kids for any length of time, since neither one of us has extended-family support, is next to impossible. That's one reason we wanted a big family, with the hope that the children will be that kind of support for each other when the time comes. Thank God for Grandma. She seemed to always be there when we needed her. No excuses, just there. Whenever Gloria was in the hospital, she was there to nurse her back to health. Alternatively, if Gloria was out of town on business, Grandma would come down to give me a hand because she knew I was hopeless without Gloria. As young as Grandma claimed to be, her true age was beginning to show. Therefore, I was reluctant to even ask her to watch the children, but we really needed this respite. Off we went to Texas, a business trip for Gloria that I accompanied her on. We weren't there twenty-four hours when the telephone rang. It was Grandma calling from our house to inform us that there was a big problem. In the background, I could hear glass smashing onto the floor and objects crashing against the wall. Shane Rico was out of control. I instructed her to have David contain him and call the police. Never would I have imagined the need to call the police on my own child, but it was necessary to protect him and everyone else in the house.

When the police arrived, I told them over the phone that, because my wife and I were away, my son needed to be removed from the house. The police officer said they would take him to the Juvenile Detention Center. Then, at my request, they put my son on the phone; he was sobbing uncontrollably. as reassuring with a tone as I could muster, I told him we would straighten this all out when I got back home, but for now, because he could not keep himself safe, he had to go with the policeman. Like a wounded lamb, he said okay. The next morning I was on a plane headed home. My other son David did all he could to clean up the residual damage and evidence of Shane Rico's rage. Nevertheless, there was no hiding it. Everything had changed. Our family would never be the same.

Our medical insurance did not cover the long-term residential treatment Shane Rico needed. After moving from Prince George's County, where services were abundant, to Fairfax County, where services were talked about but nonexistent, we were told first by a social worker that he would get the comprehensive help needed only if charged and convicted of assaulting his siblings. Then the county would be obligated to assist through the Family Resource Assistance Team, to help us out. When I arrived at the courthouse, the detective assured me that having him adjudicated would enable him to receive comprehensive psychiatric services. *What's that about? Let's lock them up to make them eligible for treatment.* What's the real motivation here? I should have been much more suspicious when the court social worker asked me "Why would you want to keep a kid like this anyway?"

"What?" I responded. "Because he's my kid!"

Next thing I know, when I read the record, she had written in the notes that I hadn't resolved my foster care issues. Imagine that, the power of the pen. She didn't expect me to read that, I'm sure. Unfortunately, I saw it after I agreed to let them charge my son as a criminal. To see him hauled away in handcuffs and brought back and forth into court that way was heartbreaking to both his mother and me. As a parent, I was ashamed, remorseful, and felt that I failed him. What was even worse, none of the services they promised was ever delivered. After attending meeting after meeting, opening ourselves up to inquiry after inquiry, as if Shane Rico was the only child we had at home, and adhering to the requirements of the county meetings and hearings, our son received not one county service. In fact, they demanded that the District of Columbia either pay for his care under the adoption subsidy agreement, which the city initially refused to honor, or the county was going to remand Shane Rico to foster care and come after us for the board rate. The latter option would have bankrupted us and put the rest of the children at risk. This could not be happening, I thought. I went to the District of Columbia Child and Family Services, which was under receivership at the time. I threatened to call a press conference, if that's what it took, and we fortunately got to a place where they reexamined their obligation under the subsidy agreement and decided that it was in all of our best interests for them to honor it. CFSA has had a leadership change since then, and is currently being led by a very capable and energetic visionary.

After years of driving three hours every other weekend to visit Shane Rico in Pennsylvania, we found a place much closer to home. Fortunately, we were able to visit him every Sunday and sometimes during the week. Gloria would drop by for lunch as often as her schedule permitted. Over time, we noticed significant improvement in his behavior. I'm sure the increased visits had plenty to do with that. In fact, he did so well, he started earning passes for home visits. However, his probation officer would not authorize him to leave the facility. I hit the roof. "That's where I draw the line," I remember saying. I informed the hospital that I was no longer authorizing the probation officer to review any information in my son's medical record if it's going to be used for punitive reasons, which can be a direct contradiction to his therapeutic needs. Well, that was the beginning of the next world war. I had no idea what I was in for. The probation officer subpoenaed me into court along with the CEO of the hospital. Again, cash-strapped from other associated expenses, I entered the courtroom with only faith as my legal counsel.

Shane Rico was represented by the county attorney. I thought it was amusing that my son had an attorney but I was there protecting his interest without one. The probation officer pleaded his case to the judge regarding the importance of access to the medical record. I responded.

The judge began lecturing me from the bench, saying that probation was the only way that a 16-year-old child is going to comply with treatment.

After initially being polite and not getting my point through, with nothing to lose, I interrupted the judge and said, "Your Honor, you are obviously not hearing me."

There was dead silence in the courtroom. Even I thought to myself, "Oh"…but I got the courage from somewhere to go on and say, "That's what he has parents for."

Then I reminded the judge that we brought this matter before the court. And that the only reason we did that was that we were told that was the way to get him the care he needed. "Well, Your Honor," I went on to say, "He hasn't received any of the care they promised and I'm asking you in light of those facts to close this case."

It was obvious that the judge was caught off guard.

"You mean the incident happened in your home?"

"Yes, You're Honor," I replied.

"You brought the matter before the court?"

"Yes, You're Honor."

With gavel in hand, he uttered, "Case dismissed!"

A loud outburst from Gloria was heard as tears fell from her eyes. The CEO of the hospital was crying. They kept saying I was awesome. I felt like some kind of hero for a minute, but I knew whom the real hero was. It was someone much bigger than me. This was a miracle. I could not even remember what I said, or where the words came from. I was happy that a wrong was made right, and all of those county workers were finally out of our lives. We could now focus exclusively on our son's healing.

While I initially struggled, in fact I was downright angry many days. At first, I asked God "Why me? Why, after all that I have already been through in my own childhood, would you have me endure this with my son's adoption?" I asked him in my private moments how he would expect me to continue to use my life this way, motivating people to adopt, when this is the experience my son and family had to endure?

After years of agony and pain, the answer came. There was purpose in my pain. It would be very easy, given all that I experienced as a child in foster care, to ask people to adopt or give a child what I never had and always wanted. It's another for me to have lived an adoption experience rooted in love, disappointment, heartache and triumph and learn from it. Then, after all of that, go out and say, when it's at its worst, don't you dare give up! You may get tired, you might burn out and have to take a break, but don't you dare give up! You may have to parent some of our special-needs adopted children unconventionally like you would a special-needs birth child that can't be cared for at home, but you never stop being a parent. That was the powerful lesson reinforced through my experience with Shane Rico, Jr.

Shane Rico is now an adult, working with computers, living in New York and doing unbelievably well. It meant the world to him knowing that although he wasn't able to live at home, somewhere to someone, he mattered. He knew he had a family who cared enough to come visit him consistently, advocate for him vigorously, and love him unconditionally. Every child deserves at least that much.

For all he's had to overcome to get where he is, I am so proud of him. So many youth his age have had so much more and thrown it away. He's using everything he has and making the most with it.

In the middle of Shane Rico's drama, my brother KB came to stay with us. He offered, in exchange, to help around the house and watch the children. It turned out not to be quite that simple. I received a call alerting me that my other brother, my father's son David, had been arrested in New York. This was of particular concern to me because it wasn't long before that I had driven up for David's junior high school graduation when he was fourteen. During that time, I tried to convince his grandmother to let him come live with me because I was deeply troubled by the crows he was associating with and his defeatist attitude. Someone asked him after graduation where his father was. I quietly watched as David responded, "He's dead."

Dad's absence hurt David deeply.

I asked him, why did he say that?

"You could come all the way from Maryland, Shane, but our so-called father couldn't come from Harlem up to the Bronx for my graduation."

Each promise our father made and didn't keep had taken a toll and hurt David a little more than the previous one. David was becoming increasingly sad, hopeless, and filled with rage. His capacity to dream of life beyond the projects of Mott Haven was diminished by the countless number of hardened friends he associated with. I told his grandmother, Ms. Jones, that it was time for him to be around a consistent positive male role model, but she refused to let him live with me. She needed him to help with his two other sisters and cousin, who were also being raised in her two-bedroom apartment. David was sixteen now, and had already been arrested. He was almost certainly on his way to Rikers Island.

We were at a crossroads. David was no longer listening to his grandmother. He was going and coming as he pleased, and now he was facing jail time. I went to New York to speak to the judge on his behalf. I promised the court that New York would never have a problem with David again, if he would allow me the chance to intervene. I asked him to release David into my custody and let him move with me to Maryland. The judge said yes, and finally his grandmother agreed to let him live with my family.

Soon after David's arrival, Gloria and I learned that he drank very heavily almost every day, and that was unacceptable. We enrolled him into a G.E.D. program. We monitored his every movement, so much, so that he called his grandmother and told her that he thought I hated him. However, unlike my brother KB, David was responding to my attempts to get him on track. We agreed that he would not work because we wanted his focus to be on getting his diploma. That made him miserable, but it paid off. David passed his G.E.D on his first attempt.

After he got his G.E.D., I got him a job at Children's Hospital. He promised that he would not repeat KB's mistake and put me in the position of having to explain his misconduct. He kept his promise. I heard nothing but good things about David from his supervisor. In fact, he was one of her favorite employees. Everything seemed to be going well until the night KB and David took Gloria's car without permission. To make matters worse, KB was driving without a license. I resented having to wake Gloria to go to the police station because of my brothers' irresponsibility. Fortunately for them, they got off with little more than an insignificant punishment.

David started dating a woman that I was less than thrilled about. She was nearly 40 years old and had five kids! David was only eighteen. In addition, he was refusing to follow the rules of the house, so I asked him to leave. That's when he moved in with his 40-year-old girlfriend. Soon thereafter, he was terminated from Children's Hospital.

The following day, KB took Gloria's car without asking again, and this time he hit a drunk pedestrian. I was terrified that we were going to lose everything we had, but fortunately, no lawsuit was filed against us. Clearly, it was time for KB to leave, this time for good. I gave KB a bus ticket back to North Carolina. He had only been in North Carolina a short time when he was involved in an altercation that left him near death. Someone had stabbed him multiple times and left him for dead. He survived his injuries, but I've been on pins and needles ever since that day, worrying that a call will come giving me the worst news imaginable about him. It became clear to me then that I had nothing else to offer him. *As grown men, we are responsible for our lives and the choices we make. I refuse to give any human being the power to allow the pain they've caused me to become my prison. I will not be held back from striving to be the best person I can be because I choose to hold onto what someone has done to me or not done for me. Pain can be either your prison or it can be your power. Pain can transform your life; it can be your poison or your purpose. It is all about the choice you make. Whichever one you choose, ultimately determines how much of life you will enjoy, and how much in life you will accomplish.*

After several years of working at Children's Hospital, I observed vast numbers of babies abandoned by substance-abusing parents. There was a shortage of adoptive and foster care families available for these children to live with and, as a result, they were spending the early months of their lives in hospitals. Surely, there must be something I can do, I thought.

I decided to call one of the local non-profit agencies, For Love of Children (FLOC). I told FLOC foster home recruiter Valli Matthews my story of having grown up in foster care and how much I didn't want that for these boarder babies.

The pain and consequences of not having a permanent home is something no child should experience. She invited me to go on the Cathy Hughes morning show on WOL radio in Washington, DC to help recruit families. Pleased with my performance on the radio show, Valli asked me to sit on a foster parents training panel. It wasn't long afterwards that I began to get invitations to speak at various conferences around the country where social workers, administrators, foster families, adoptive families, and youth came together to advocate for children in need of homes. My childhood psychologist, Dr. Lewis, heard that I was coming to Albany, New York, to give a speech about my experiences in foster care and wrote to me. Years later, I still have the wonderful letter she sent.

April 30, 1993

Dear Shane —

    I saw your name in the Program of "Celebrating Adoption". I would really have tried to come to hear you, but I will be out of town that week. However, I must tell you how proud I am of you, how much I admire and respect you.

    Through thick & thin, ups & downs (and there were many!) I never for a moment gave up on you or stopped thinking that you were so special. It's people like you that make my work & life so rewarding.

    Shane, I still have on my wall the "play" you wrote at 10 yrs of age called "Adopted Child". I've shown it to so many people over the years, I consider it priceless. I remember so clearly after one of your mishaps a couple of years later, your saying "I'm nobody without a family".

    I think the time has come to turn it over to you — The play I mean — for you to have and show. After all, we are all family & so should share. I would like to hear from you —— busy schedule & all —

and maybe you'll honor us with a visit to NY soon!

Take care & regards to all,

Selma Lewis

I thanked her for believing in me when no one else did and promised that I would continue to make her proud.

Dr. Lewis told me that my roommate from the Rego Park Group Home, Kenny, had asked about me, and she helped me get in touch with him. Kenny was completing graduate school in California at the time and wanted to come back east. I offered, and he accepted, an invitation to stay with my family and me.

We had a wonderful reunion, but I was shocked that, just like my brother Kenny, felt that I had abandoned him when I left the group home for college. I was clueless. I guess I never realized how much we really meant to each other, but then again when you're transitioning out of a group-home to adulthood, more often than not, you're all you got. In retrospect, I could see what he meant. All he had to do was write me and I would have definitely written back. To my knowledge, he still lives in the Washington, DC area, but we still don't keep in touch.

The speaking circuit has been a wonderful experience. I've met some fascinating people who are very committed to better outcomes for youth. I've met some wacky ones too. Many unfortunately are driven more by power and turf rather than the healing and transformation of our communities and children. It's always refreshing when I get the chance to be in the company of people who genuinely care about kids, people who are willing to transcend whatever barriers to make things right. On my way to an engagement, I had the most phenomenal reunion.

As my plane landed in Seattle, I remembered that Reverend Kennedy, my former dad, had relocated to Seattle and died of a heart attack. I decided to look up his mother and sister to see how they were doing and to let them know how I was doing. I had no idea how to get in touch with them, but I remembered that as a little boy he always talked about how great being a member of Mt. Zion Baptist Church was. I called Mt. Zion, explained that I had been one of Reverend Kennedy's foster children and recently learned of his death, and wanted to know how to reach his family.

The woman on the other end of the phone said, "Reverend Kennedy isn't dead."

He was alive, well, and working as a school principal. Talk about a surprise! I was so thrilled that Reverend Kennedy was okay, but I was also nervous about seeing him after all we'd gone through. With my friend Jackie providing moral support, I decided to pay a visit to Reverend Kennedy's school.

When he emerged from his office, he was surprised to see me. He embraced me warmly and seemed genuinely pleased to see me. We spoke briefly, and I invited him to come hear me speak. He couldn't commit but he said he would try to make it. I said good-bye to Reverend Kennedy not knowing if I'd ever see him again, but it sure felt good to let him see that I made it, that I was doing fine.

Just as I began my speech at the One Church One Child Conference, Reverend Kennedy strolled into the hotel ballroom. I was startled at first, but remained focused on my remarks. As I acknowledged him from the podium, it dawned on me that many of the rules he imposed on me that I rebelled against were the same rules that I was imposing on Tiffany. I acknowledged in my remarks that I wasn't able to receive the love he was trying to give when I was in his home. Knowing how much I still desired a relationship with a father, I asked him, "Is it too late for me to ask you to be my dad?"

"No, it's not," he said and in that moment we connected.

The impact on the others was far greater than I could have ever imagined. One minister declared that he was going to go searching for his long lost son. Father Clement committed to strengthening his relationship with his son Joey. So many fathers decided to reunite or have better relationships with their children. How powerful! What a wonderful sense of purpose that experience gave me.

Shortly after my return from Seattle, I received a late-night call from my grandmother. My Aunt Cookie (Sylvia) was found dead outside a four-story building in Harlem. Her death was treated as a homicide at first, but then authorities concluded that she might have jumped. I don't know if we'll ever know for sure. I told Grandma that I would pay for Aunt Cookie's funeral. This was my way of doing for my mother's sister what I would have wanted to do for my mom. This was my opportunity for closure. At the funeral, I saw my Aunt's son Omar for the first time in more than fourteen years. I had often asked Grandma about him, but she refused to put us in touch.

Omar was a handful, and Grandma knew I would probably try to take that responsibility on too. It turns out he was living in a group home, bitter and filled with rage. I would tell Grandma repeatedly that maybe Omar needed me. I felt I could understand what he was going through. Nevertheless, Grandma insisted that I didn't need to take on anything else.

Whether Grandma liked it or not, I was determined to speak with him. He barely remembered me, but I remembered him well. He was the oldest of Aunt Cookie's five children, all of whom were in foster care at one point or another. At first, I just promised to stay in touch with him. Then I invited him to come back to Maryland with me so that we could get to know each other better. The folks at the group home thought coming with me had to be better than what awaited

Omar back in the tough neighborhood where he lived. Omar was a tough guy, having secured a place on several "Most Wanted" neighborhood lists

After the funeral, I returned home with Omar. With a telephone number given to him by his stepfather, he hoped to reunite with his siblings. Omar was heartbroken to discover that he had a wrong number and no clue how to contact his brothers and sisters. Thank goodness, he was at my house when he realized this and not in New York by himself. There is no telling how he would have displayed his anger had I not been there for him.

I did not realize it when I invited him home, but I learned from his group home that Omar's last hope to turn his life around was a program called Glenn Mills in Pennsylvania. Gloria and I promised Omar that if he successfully completed Glenn Mills, he would always have a family standing beside him, and that as long as he was enrolled, we would visit him regularly. A little, over two years later, with all promises kept, including regular home visits with us on weekends and holidays, Omar graduated from Glenn Mills with his high school diploma and a G.E.D. Gloria and I were so proud of him, and we knew that once again we had been used to transform a life from pain to promise. When Omar came back to live with us after graduation, I helped him get a job at Children's Hospital and he performed exemplarily. Eventually he left our home and got a place of his own with his girlfriend.

My relationship with my grandmother had grown to a place where we talked every day about everything. We initially built the relationship around developing strategies to ensure that my sister successfully transitioned to adulthood. In other words, we intended to make sure she wasn't jacked up by some dude before graduating from high school. That was enough to create a strong bond between us. It wasn't very long after Omar moved out that my grandmother was fed up with my sister Shanique and sent her to live with Gloria and me. However, we were not as successful with her as we had hoped to be.

While Gloria and I were at work one day, we left Shanique to baby sit Tiffany, Shane Rico, Brittney and Courtney. When I got home from work, Shanique was nowhere to be found, and Tiffany was playing with the kitchen stove. When I confronted Shanique about her neglectful behavior, she simply shrugged her shoulders and said "So?"

I went bonkers. I had flashbacks of our mother leaving me unattended. I simply lost it. That was the end of her stay. She was back in New York in less than a week's time.

I started having an increasing desire to be closer to my grandmother for some reason. Now in my early thirties, the more I fought it, the stronger it got. I finally just gave in and acknowledged it. That's when I really began to enjoy and appreciate our relationship for everything it was, instead of grieving for all that it wasn't. We became best friends. Over time, each telephone conversation ended with me asking her when she was going to leave New York and spend some time with me. Each time she'd give me the same answer, "Oh, it won't be long," until one day, I just called and asked her again and when she gave me that usual answer, I wouldn't accept it.

I said, "Ma, all of these years, I've never needed nor asked anything from you, but I need you now. I need you to come down and be with me, let me lie in your lap like a big baby and just hold me. I need you to get to know my kids and for them to get to know you."

Not a second passed before she responded and said: "I'll be there," She came, and I did just that. After a couple of days, I put my head in her lap and just lay there. She caressed my face. And I told her how tired I was as tears started to fall. "I don't know how much more of this I can do? I've been fighting all my life to survive, trying not to repeat the mistakes of my mom and dad. But everyday it seems to get harder. It's a struggle getting through. Sometimes I'm tired of carrying this burden and feeling like nobody understands how hard it is to be me."

She softly said, "I know baby, I know."

And I just lay there quietly, for the first time since my mom walked out on me; I was being held and touched by a parent. There was a strange sensation that let me know, I 'm human.

Never again did I have to ask more than once; Mom's visits became steady. My home was her second home her escape from New York."

She began to change, to soften and open up, as we spent time together. We both did. I laughed with her and teased her about her weight, and she teased me about mine. It's somewhat funny, everything I hoped to find in all those homes, I ultimately found with my grandmother. The woman who at first rejected me. I often wonder what my life would have been like if I just left her alone, not pursued her. I would have never experienced the beauty and strength of our relationship. My children's lives know what it means to have a resident grandmother. Grandma doesn't miss anything, and they don't like that at all.

I got a call from a friend who worked at the local Child and Family Services agency. She said, they had a kid who would be perfect for our family. This kid had been featured on a local television newscast. She sent me a copy of the videotape, and as soon as Gloria and I saw it, we fell in love with 14-year-old David.

Grandma was visiting at the time so I asked her what she thought, and she said, "If I could raise six, you can raise five."

Probably not the best response to listen to, I thought. I asked Tiffany about her feelings and she responded just as a teenage girl would, "he's cute; I'll be very popular at school."

The most moving part of the tape was when the reporter asked David why, at fourteen, he still wanted to be adopted.

"When I'm thirty years old, I'm going to want a place to bring my children back to," David said.

I was thirty at the time and I had no place to bring my children back to. I felt an instant connection to him. The rest of the family saw the tape, we talked it over, and everybody agreed that David should become a part of our family. It was a unanimous decision. We didn't tell any of our friends or extended family right away because we feared that they would try to discourage us from adopting a 14-year-old black male, especially with three girls at home.

When my father-in-law found out about our plans, he asked, "What the hell are you trying to do to my daughter? Don't you all have enough kids?"

I simply responded by telling him that he was selling himself short if he believed he had raised a child who wasn't an independent thinker. In fact, it was because of the gift of adoption he gave her that she felt so compelled to give others the same. After that, he never uttered a word on the subject again. Born David Lewis, our son became David Lenard Aytch Salter through adoption. Gloria and I were thrilled that we were able to give a home to another child branded "hard to place." Now David would have somewhere to bring his children back to when he's thirty.

8

OUR SONG

○ ○

I know your image of me is what I hope to be, I've treated you unkindly, but you can see, there's no one else important to me, can't you see through me—You taught me precious secrets of a true love withholding nothing, you came out in front when I was hiding, and now, I'm so much better.
A. Nesby

It's unbelievable to me. Somewhat of a fantasy at times. Watching her and my children interact. Hearing them call her Grandma and being scolded by her from time to time. Seeing my wife being able to rely on her consistently for occasional respite. What I wasn't able to receive in my childhood, I'm now beginning to experience with my children, wife and grandmother: experience family.

At times, it's as if we're inseparable, and then at times, when my moods kick in, I feel claustrophobic, like I'm suffocating. Those moments pass quickly, though. One thing is for sure, Shane loves his Grandma and Grandma sure loves her some Shane.

Not many people, given our history, understand how our relationship evolved to this. Some immediate and extended family members even resent it because they think it's without merit. Yes, I drop everything when she calls. And as long as I'm aware of it, her every need is attended to. You could say time heals wounds, but that would be too trite. It's more than that. I prefer the Covey principle, "Seek first to understand, before seeking to be understood." I try to live by that in all that I do. When I have turned away from something or someone, it is because I have exhausted my capacity for understanding and found malice of heart or intent.

Spending the years with my grandmother since graduating from high school enabled her to be honest and forthcoming with the facts surrounding her feelings, choices and circumstances leading up to and after my birth. For that, I grew to understand and respect her. Through oral history, she has helped me understand who I am and made it impossible for others to define me. As I recount some of what she shared with me, perhaps you too might understand the multigenerational pain that contributed to the abandonment of my six-month-old baby brother and me when I was just four years old, and why I was so determined to try breaking the cycle with my children, my siblings, and my cousins.

You see, Sherry's grandmother Flossy was a New York City showgirl. It was her goal-driven, succeed-at-any-cost attitude that made her walk away from her infant daughter and husband to further her showgirl career with the merchant marines. On a blustery winter day, she wrapped Sandra warmly in her bassinet before leaving the child on the doorstep of her Aunt Gertie. Flossy walked away and never looked back. Gertie was shocked that Flossy would do such a thing, but she was happy to have Sandra to raise as her own.

Sandra grew up following her mother's colorful career. Meanwhile, Flossy showed no interest in her. In fact, she appeared to go out of her way to act is if Sandra had never been born. It shattered Sandra's heart to think that the woman who gave birth to her could deny her, especially since Sandra had done nothing to deserve such rejection. Aunt Gertie did her best to counteract the damage Flossy's rejection had done. As often as possible, she reassured Sandra that she was beautiful, and told her repeatedly that she could be anything she wanted to be. She could even be a showgirl just like her mother if she wanted. "I'll be anything but like my mother," Sandra insisted. The years of abandonment and neglect changed Sandra's feelings for her mother from disappointment to hatred. However, she adored her Aunt Gertie, and Sandra was devastated when Gertie died suddenly. Sandra was eighteen, and the only mother she had ever known was gone. Sandra was alone, scared, broke, and had no marketable skills other than the domestic abilities she had acquired at home. In her vulnerable state, the first man who came along—Leroy, a high yellow brother with freckles—had no trouble charming the stockings off her. Their marriage didn't last. Leroy was abusive to Sandra from the start. When Sandra returned home from the hospital after having their first child, Leroy raped her, rupturing her so terribly she had to be rushed back to the hospital. The doctors and nurses couldn't believe the damage Leroy's attack had done.

Sandra eventually left Leroy and moved to New Jersey, but it wasn't long before she took Leroy back and allowed him and his mother to move in with her. That turned out to be the worst mistake of her life. Leroy drank excessively and beat her up regularly. She didn't know which was more painful, getting her ass beat or the humiliation of Leroy's mother looking on with approval.

"A man's got to do what a man's got to do," his mother would say.

Sandra always knew that Leroy's mother felt that she wasn't good enough for him, and finally Sandra had come to the conclusion that her mother-in-law was right. She didn't deserve Leroy and she didn't deserve to be abused. However, Sandra didn't think she could do much better than Leroy could, so she tried to make the marriage work. Mostly, she stayed because she didn't want to abandon her child the way her mother, Flossy, had abandoned her.

Confused and conflicted, Sandra had another child with Leroy after. She left him again, but he found out where she was living, kicked in the door, and carried her and the two children back to New Jersey, where they sold bootleg liquor for a living. Their third child, my mother Sherry, was born shortly thereafter.

Sandra and Leroy and their three children eventually moved to Hartford, Connecticut. During an argument, Leroy threw his wife out of a moving car, and she rolled down into a ditch. A passerby saved her life by calling an ambulance. The only good thing about that incident was that Leroy never found her again. Sandra didn't know if Leroy hadn't found her because he thought she was dead or if he were afraid, she would call the police. Whatever the reason, she was at last free of Leroy.

Sandra moved in with the grandmother, met a new love, and had her fourth child. She became an erotic dancer to feed her children. While dancing in nightclubs she met a sailor named Eric and had her fifth and sixth children with him. Eventually Sandra got her own place in the South Bronx.

Although she was a single mother of six now, Sandra still thought she was a little hot thing. Her new boyfriend, Vernon, must have thought so too, because he would think nothing of jumping on the subway from the Upper Westside for an occasional booty call. In addition, she didn't take any stuff from nobody, especially when it came to protecting her kids. It was not unusual to see Sandra in the street fighting someone who messed over one of her kids. Life had taught her that families stick together and that they defend each other no matter what. She made sure all the kids were reminded of that every day before they walked out the door.

It was no secret that her boys were her favorites. Her sons could do no wrong. However, when it came to her daughter, Sherry, she was particularly protective. I guess you have to be when your daughter is one of the prettiest girls in the neighborhood and, at thirteen, one of the last remaining virgins. Every little roughneck in the neighborhood had staked his claim to Sherry.

At 13 years old, Sherry was arrested for stealing, but Sandra was certain that Sherry was set up, never for one minute doubting her innocence.

The detective was hauling Sherry off in handcuffs when he accidentally hit her in the eye. Instinctively and with no regard for the fact that the officer was carrying a gun, Sandra picked up the closest frying pan and hit him upside his head. All hell broke loose, and in the end, both mother and daughter were handcuffed and taken to the police station. The judge released Sandra, but sent Sherry away for a year to Hudson Juvenile Home for Girls.

After Sherry was released from Hudson, Sandra really tightened the reins on her, refusing to let Sherry out of her sight. Boyfriends were out of the question for Sherry until Sandra's boyfriend Vernon suggested that he introduce Sherry to his little brother David. With Sherry always in the house, Vernon couldn't get enough "private time" with her mother. David could keep Sherry busy, while Vernon got busy with Sandra. At first, Sandra wasn't too keen on the idea. "I ain't having any stuff up in here, Sandra warned."

"You don't have a thing to worry about," Vernon assured her. "Dee Dee ain't nothing to worry about and you know I'll jack him up if he tries anything. Besides, it's time for Sherry to have a little freedom; you can't keep that girl locked up like that."

Eventually, Vernon got his way and Sandra allowed Dee Dee to come around with Vernon and keep Sherry company.

Dee Dee turned on the charm and hit it off with Sandra right away. His gift of gab gave her the impression that he was a good kid. The truth of the matter was that 16-year-old Dee Dee was nothing but a smooth-talking, dope-dealing hustler and a master thief. In his short life, he had already spent as much time in juvenile detention as he had spent at home. Sherry found his charm irresistible, and none of the other boys in the neighborhood stood a chance after that. When Dee Dee discovered that Sherry was not only beautiful, but could sing too, he melted like butter. It wasn't long after she met Dee Dee that Sherry was in love, surrendered her virginity, and become pregnant with me. It all happened with Vernon and Sandra locked in the next room, too busy with each other to realize I was being conceived on the living room couch.

Sherry was terrified when she found out she was pregnant, not so much about the baby, but her mother's response. She knew that Sandra had big dreams for her daughter. The thought of Sherry repeating her mother's mistakes was unacceptable. Sherry couldn't stop thinking about all the times her mother had warned her not to get pregnant and what she threatened to do if any daughter of hers dared to disobey.

"You better not bring any babies up in here. If any of you come in here pregnant, I'm telling you, I'll beat it out of you."

If there was one thing Sherry knew about her mother it was that she said what she meant, and meant what she said. She had to keep her pregnancy a secret from her mother for her own safety and the safety of her baby.

A neighbor finally gave away Sherry's secret. She commented to Sandra that Sherry seemed to be getting a bit big and asked, "Are you sure she ain't pregnant?"

"Hell no! I don't let that girl out of my sight," Sandra insisted. "Besides, she knows I'd beat her ass down if she tried to come in here with a baby."

But later that evening, as soon as Sherry walked in the door, Sandra made Sherry take off her clothes, and there was no doubt that Sherry was very pregnant. The sight of Sherry's bulging tummy sent Sandra into a hysterical rage. She started pounding on Sherry with her fists and screaming at the top of her lungs, "I'm gonna beat you till it drops out of you."

Sherry fell to the floor and curled herself into a knot, trying desperately to protect her baby from her mother's punches, kicks, and stomps, crying and begging her to stop. It seemed the beating was never going to end until finally, exhausted and out of breath, Sandra stopped. The terrible beating she took from her mother was surely enough to cause Sherry to miscarry, but, amazingly, both the baby and Sherry survived. I had won my very first fight for survival.

Having failed in her attempt to beat the baby out of her daughter, Sandra plotted to have Sherry's pregnancy terminated.

"...You, you are not bringing no baby in here, we are getting rid of it."

She made an appointment and dragged Sherry to an illegal, backdoor abortion house. They had only just begun prepping her for the procedure, when Sherry jumped off the table, grabbed her clothes, and bolted out of the door.

"You are not going to kill my baby," she screamed and ran from the abortion house, running and putting on her clothes at the same time. Sandra eventually had to accept the fact that Sherry was determined to keep her baby, and that I was going to be born.

Things didn't look good at all when the time came for Sherry to deliver. She was just 15 years old, with blood pressure so high the doctors didn't think she would survive the birth. They could save the baby, they thought. A priest was called to perform last rites. Sandra nearly collapsed when she heard this. She couldn't believe it was happening—her daughter was near death giving birth to a child she never wanted. She went to the chapel and prayed for Sherry's life.

"God, if you have to take one off them, please take this baby and let Sherry live," she pleaded. And God did what she asked, and more.

Sherry miraculously survived the life-threatening complications, and on November 21, 1963, at 11:20pm, I was born as David Earl Williams Jr. weighing in at 7 pounds, 11 ounces. My name was changed from David to Shane, thanks to Grandma Sandra's refusal to have me named after my father. Sandra hated my father so much that she told the hospital records clerk that she would "kick her ass" if David Williams showed up on that birth certificate. Wisely, the terrified clerk chose not to risk a confrontation and issued my birth certificate with the name Shane Lenard Salter, per my grandmother's instructions. Shane was inspired by the old western starring Alan Ladd, and Lenard was in reverence to my uncle, John Lenard. Shane, a variation of John, means God's most gracious gift. In Hebrew, it means beautiful.

A few years after I was born, my mother applied for public assistance and we moved to our own apartment in the basement of a brownstone in Harlem. It was my father, Dee Dee, who introduced my mother to drugs, which eventually led to her heroin addiction. With Dee Dee in and out of jail, my mother met Norman, a much older man who tried unsuccessfully to help her get off drugs. It was Norman who fathered my mother's second son, KB, who was born in 1966.

Of course, I knew none of this while growing up. All I knew was that my family wasn't there. I didn't understand for many years what happened to my mother or why she didn't come back for us. Now I know, and I understand. While I don't excuse or justify my mother's actions, I certainly understand her pain and I understand how this could happen against her best intentions. I have learned from seeing the pain in my grandmother's eyes from the abandonment she experienced as a little girl dropped off on a doorstep, that it's so hard to give what you didn't get or what you don't have. Familial child abuse and neglect in the family is largely an intergenerational problem. Although it is clear that the nature and degree of some types of abuse is reflective of severe mental illness or character disorders, many abusive parents of abused and neglected children were abused themselves and are attempting, to the best of their ability, to cope with environmental stresses and the demands of parenting. It was this depth of understanding that opened the door for true forgiveness and helped me recognize and confront my own demons.

9

YOU WERE LOVED

o o o o o o o o o o o o o o o o o o o o o o o o o o o o o o o o o o

you were loved by someone, touched by someone, held by someone,
meant something to someone, loved somebody,
touched somebody's heart along the way,
you can look back and say....you did ok, you were loved.
W. Houston

On Christmas night 1999, I received a call from Mom Jamison telling me that her son Robbie had died. When I offered to come home to be with her and the family, I was mystified when she told me not to.

"It's the holiday; we can't do anything right now. I'll call you with the arrangements."

A few days later, she left a voicemail, referring to herself as "Doris," which was very strange. She was always "Mom" to "Grandma and me" to my children, never "Doris." Perhaps it was just the stress of it all. I conceded when she asked me to write Robbie's obituary. I was so excited to know I could be of some value that somehow I might fit in. I went to work on it right away. I was so proud of what I wrote and eager to show it to her. She became surprisingly irritated that I stated in my first draft that Robbie had died "after a long illness."

"Take that out," she snapped.

I was puzzled. It was a long illness. I put my feelings aside. He was *her* son, and I wasn't supposed to be grieving; he was no longer my brother.

During the funeral, when I placed a hand on her back to comfort her, she whispered, "Don't touch me."

At that point, I knew she was angry with me, but I had no idea why.

On the way from the cemetery, after Robbie's burial, I asked Mom Jamison if I could have a small token from Robbie's apartment as a keepsake, and she snapped at me again. "He didn't have anything; I don't know what you want."

At that point, I decided it was best not to say anything more to her. That's when it hit me. She was angry because it was Robbie and not I who had died. I was not supposed to be the one who survived. I was not supposed to be the one who completed college. Mom and Dad Jamison meant the world to me. I knew that I wouldn't have survived without them, and I thought I meant just as much to them. I was so endeared and never missed an opportunity to show the depth of my gratitude.

It seemed that I was stuck in time. They were still my parents, but I was their former foster child. Mom Jamison and I didn't speak at all until five years later when I happened to run into her at a wedding in Washington. After posing together for a couple of pictures, I gave her a hug, looked her dead in the eye, and told her, "No matter what, I still love you and there's nothing you can do about it."

Her only response was, "You're squishing my glasses."

After Robbie's death, Dad Jamison took seriously ill, which, sadly, meant that Mom Jamison was spending all of her retirement years caring for the two men in her house who were gravely ill; first her son, and then her husband.

I finally got up the nerve to call her, we actually had a good conversation about everything except the reason we didn't talk all those years. We aren't quite back to our old relationship yet, but I think the healing process has begun. I just don't have the energy I used to, to be the driver in relationships. I noticed a pattern over the years: As with most of my relationships it seems, if I don't initiate contact, the relationship eventually dwindles. Well lately, I've just let this one and a lot of others die. It feels rotten when I'm doing the calling and visiting all the time. I had to do that as a kid in order to keep a roof over my head. As an adult, well that is what is great about being an adult, no more begging for unconditional love and acceptance. I am learning to unconditionally love and accept my own self, which is good enough for now.

At first, after I ran away from my father, I was too afraid to visit him. I heard that he was stabbed nine times while I was at Elmira College, and almost lost his life. When I returned from school and visited him, he drove me by an abandoned building in the Bronx. "The bodies of the men who tried to kill me are in that building," he boasted, pointing at the dilapidated garden apartment.

In addition to all of his other crimes, I couldn't believe he was claiming to be a murderer. I watched him deteriorate over the years and increasingly lost respect for him. After my first daughter, Tiffany, was born, I refused to call him Dad and started calling him by his nickname, Dee Dee. Now that I was a father, with my own vision of what a father should be, I couldn't bring myself to call him Dad anymore. As I matured and grew spiritually, I found myself compelled to, "Honor thy Father and thy Mother." I recognize that we are not commanded to honor thy father and thy mother if they fail to measure up to our expectations. I also realized that at the end of my own earthly journey, I won't be judged by what kind of father I had, but rather by what kind of son I was. After that revelation, our relationship improved significantly, as we developed a new love and respect for one another. When my father died, while I loved him, I felt relieved.

His youngest child at the time of his death was two years old. I vowed no more siblings of mine would enter the foster care system or become addicted to drugs.

I always knew I would be responsible for his funeral arrangements, and although finances were very tight in my house at the time, I did my duty. None of his siblings or family members would contribute to the expenses for one reason or another. I asked a friend, an ordained minister, to ride with me from Washington, DC and to preside at his service.

When she asked me what she should know about him, I told her the truth: My father had been a thief, drug dealer, drug addict, and possibly a murderer, few if any of the things a father ought to be. I insisted that her eulogy be honest. His sister did agree to dress him in a short sleeve golf shirt, pants and tennis shoes. Just the way he looked every day. He never looked more peaceful; not a gray hair in his head and his skin as smooth as silk. At the service, the minister did just as I asked, and, to my surprise, the funeral was hilarious. No one expected me to keep it that real. Yet, because we did so, everyone could appreciate and recognize the person we were talking about, and the soul we were praying for. The minister did an awesome job.

This stuff led my great-grandmother to beg me to live my life, leave my family alone and never look back. She told me that this estranged family of mine was only going to bring me down. However, it's not my nature to turn my back on folks that I care about, so I continued to pursue relationships with her and as many other members of my family as I could find. When great-grandmother died, sadly, she had lost most of her material wealth by the time she passed away. She entrusted her possessions to a friend as she became less mobile. Given the non-existent relationship with my grandmother and no one else to rely on, this friend robbed her blind. Even the baby grand was gone. However, it was equally painful to watch my great-granddad slip away. Toward the end of his life, he developed Alzheimer's. As a result, he wasn't able to recognize me when I visited him in the hospital. Just think he was the only one who made me believe I was remembered while in foster care, and now, he didn't know me anymore. That was hard. However, it didn't take long for me to realize, every time I look at that old baby shoe, I would never forget how he remembered me and believed in me when it mattered most. While seeing him like this was painful, the condition he was in was not reflective of the relationship we had. I found my peace and accepted that great-granddad was leaving us, one day at a time. It was not long before he peacefully closed those bright eyes for the last time and left for his final journey.

As for KB, we don't have a relationship. It's amazing; to have been so close as kids, now we were like Cain and Able. After numerous attempts to work on a relationship, with the result always the same, I've just let it go an unfortunate casualty of this experience. However, I respect him for all that he has endured and accomplished in spite of. He's fighting the good fight and I'm proud of him for that.

My sister Shanique lives in New York with her beautiful son, Shalik. I'm so proud of the woman she's become, we have a healthy relationship.

My brother David went to technical school and became a certified cable installer. David has worked for Verizon for over six years. He and his wife own their own home in Maryland. I can't help but chuckle as I watch him repeatedly open his doors to relatives and friends down on their luck. A chip off the old block if I must say so myself.

Aunt Cookie's son, Omar is now working for the Department of the Treasury in Washington, DC, and is the father of four children.

The Moorages, my unofficial foster parents, have retired and now live in Greenwood, South Carolina. It was Dad Moorages, in fact, who gave me the initial inspiration when I was 17 to share this journey with the public as an opportunity for learning and healing. Just graduating from high school, after all he witnessed I had gone through, was a miracle, he told me. "You're supposed to do something with all of this, write it down, people need to know about it," he went on to say. I never forgot those words, and promised him I would write a book some day.

Reverend Kennedy relocated to Washington, is adopting two more children, and playing an active role in my life as friend, Dad and Grandpa to my children. We have a great adult relationship. He is a complex person yet straightforward. I understand him much better now and love him for his heart and the sincerity of his intentions. What we were unable to have when I was a kid; we are enjoying two fold as adults.

I never saw Mr. Pointer again. I tried searching for him. People I've met on the speaking circuit have also offered to search for him in all kinds of creative ways. I wish he could have seen the man I've become after all the heartache I caused and the time he invested. He was a powerful social worker with a profound impact on my life.

For the longest time I was resigned to the fact that what happened to me growing up was just an experience. It just happened, so what. I went on with life as if everything was okay. Then when the voice inside me said that there was a purpose for my pain, I listened, and then asked what could be the purpose? I saw no real value, but the voice within me said the purpose was healing. What? Yes, there's healing in the pain. Then I realized my responsibility to share my experience so that others might have an opportunity for their own healing or to help someone else with theirs. I had a testimony. It was a testimony to what others discard for trash, God means for treasure. I believe that we each have purpose, every child has purpose, and every child has potential. Sadly, many of our children have pain that's become the prison locking up their potential; consequently, their life purpose is devalued. We can and must do better than this for all of our children; at the very least, for those in harms way.

After running myself ragged for years, I realized that in order to be complete, I had to confront my pain and claim my "get out of prison" card. The real work required me to stop running and start looking, listening and learning who I am. As I've begun this self exploration, many things have been uncovered…I thought initially since I didn't turn out so bad, the system must have been okay with a few hic cups here and there. It wasn't until I started engaging in dialog with my grown daughter Tiffany and my other children, and looking over the course of my life at the relationships I've been unable to sustain, both personally and professionally, that I realized the price I've paid as a result of years and years of childhood rejection, abuse and neglect. All the years I thought I knew what love is, and all the years I thought I was giving love to those that mattered most to me, only to painfully realize, I was repeating the cycle of neglect and abuse; only mine was the worse neglect of them all, it was emotional. I fought all my life not to abandon Tiffany, associating success with breaking the cycle with physical abandonment, not walking out on her the way my parents walked out on me. Never knowing because I never had it myself, that it is so much more than just being physically present. The other lesson I learned is cute little babies grow up. Some of them turn into teenagers you don't recognize. Therefore, it's not about needing love in return. I remember when I had feelings as a little boy, and I remember when I stopped feeling. Now it is my one desire to learn how to love me so that I can love my family and others that are important to me. My grandmother opened the door for me the day she rocked me in her arms, laid my head on her lap and simply said, "I know baby, I know." She knew that all my life I just wanted to know what love felt like. I longed to be wanted, understood, and connected. Something I lost early, something all the moves from home to home deprived me of. When grandma said, "I know…I know," stroking my face gently, and repeatedly saying, "I know." I did not understand how much she meant what she said, until I learned her story. Then I suddenly realized, her story was my story and my pain was our common understanding. Light bulbs started flashing as I looked in her glazed eyes and saw all the years of heartache, disappointment, and broken dreams riding so heavy on her back. Her pain became her poison, and she too was imprisoned by it. However, the gates were opening for both of us, and the opportunity for healing unfolded. I opened my heart wide, and love came dancing into my soul for the very first time. Therefore, she struggled trying to give what she thought was love to her children, only to realize in so many ways that what she gave, was not what they needed most. Up until recently, I was doing the same. Fortunately, I have the chance to continue working on this path to healing. Grandma doesn't.

My grandmother died on Christmas Eve. She was taken to the hospital while in New York. Her daughter Jewel didn't want me there and started a family conspiracy to encourage others not to call me, so they didn't until it was too late. While on Amtrak, I received a spiteful call from Jewel, informing me grandma died an hour before. It was just as grandma and I predicted it would happen if she were survived by her daughter. I have tried to reconcile that experience by accepting that Jewel and the others obviously needed that time with her more than I did. I often teased grandma by begging her not to leave me here to deal with her daughter and family around her arrangements. However, I told her "if you happen to leave first, count on the fact that when I put your remains in the ground, so goes the relationships I have with the rest of this family. I won't let them do to me what they've done to you." She sat quietly, I do not think she quite approved, but she certainly understood. Grandma and I always said to each other, if either one of us went today or tomorrow, there was nothing left to be said. We'd laugh and say, there should be no "boo hooing" and "falling out" over caskets, because all of our love was expressed while we lived. There is no reason for either of us to second-guess the depth of our love, we often reminded each other. Well, I should have known grandma would have the last word regardless. In the box with her burial papers, I was instructed to distribute letters she wrote and left to the people addressed on the envelopes after I finished all the arrangements…My letter is copied as she wrote it:

Hi Darling:

I know that this is a sad time for you, You know baby, that you are my first grand-child, my best friend, we could talk & say anything to each other, I love you & have loved you, more then you will ever know, but you have known that, you know that you are my baby + you have given me so much joy, You have made me so proud of you. Also, you gave me my flowers when I was around, all the time, never was there ever anything, that ever you thought I wanted or needed that you didn't make it possible, there I love you so much, I haven't baby left you, just look + you will see me smile, One day we will be together again, I'll always be around you the bond is there + it always will be. When you play that song Precious Lord, think of me, that of me when you made me laugh, + when you said silly things to me, Be strong, take care of your-self + family I love you so much. Love you "

Mom "

There is no amount of money she could have ever left me that would give me what that letter did. To think, when she started coming to visit me in Maryland, then Virginia and DC, she was not going to church and her faith relationship was weak to say the least. Through Gloria and me, she developed a relationship with our pastor, attended church regularly, and before she departed, she had the chance to ask God's forgiveness as she said with her final words "for any wrong I've ever done" and then everyone in the room told me her last word was Hallelujah! You see that is why you will hear me say from time to time, Trouble will come and Trouble will go, but the one thing about Trouble is...Trouble Don't Last Always!

10

TROUBLE DON'T LAST

o o o o o o o o o o o o o o o o o o o o o o o o o o o o o o o o o o

Just another baby born…stuck in the ghetto cement. to a teen
mom
given no support, no hope, and no encouragement.
when they wrote him off could they have thought?
that baby boy someday would walk
among children, mayors and presidents.

Who ever thought when they passed him by?
pretending as if they did not hear him cry
the boy would become man and return to say
I made it, and still I rise.

Who would have thought, the one they rejected
would find his voice among the abused and neglected?
who would have thought out of so much pain?
God would give purpose…and call him Shane.

There are many little Shanes along your way
just stop, look…and listen…you will hear them say…
Wake Up, don't forget me, I need you today
without your help, I might go astray.
If you don't just look the other way
you will be proud knowing someday
when you woke up, you helped me say
I made it, I did ok
Then I will rise, and then I will say…
because you cared, *trouble "did not" last always.*

My professional career in child welfare began with serving as chief operating officer at For Love of Children (FLOC). FLOC was one of the largest family support nonprofits in Washington, DC. This was an opportunity for me to develop patience, confront the realities of how the system really worked, and to see the worst and best in people, all in the name of serving children.

Life came full circle when I realized that now, as a child welfare administrator, I was not the kid who returned from college to the group home and learned he had no bed because it was given to a new resident. I was presiding over the system that gives those beds away in order to "ensure maximum census for full reimbursement." In other words, my decisions were driven by how many kids we had in our foster homes, and how many we had in our group homes, to ensure I could meet payroll. The numbers of kids coming back to the agency in need of support or additional resources after being discharged from our program disheartened me because we had no additional services to offer them. Is it no wonder that 45 percent of those leaving foster care became homeless within a year?

The CEO and I were as different as day and night. He was an incredible visionary from Kentucky and I was an Urban Cowboy from the South Bronx. Fred, my supervisor, is a passionate, no-frills advocate for children. I learned so much working with him.

After my tenure with FLOC, I went to serve as the national director of the Marriott Foundation for People with Disabilities. It was my introduction to corporate America. What a challenge it was transitioning from a non-profit, where the prevailing sentiment was "can't we all just get along," to Marriott, where although we were running a non-profit, I was regularly reminded we were running a business that must be reflective of the Marriott Corporation standard.

Shortly after arriving, the CEO took me to meet Richard Marriott, and introduced me as the new national director. In customary fashion, I shook Mr. Marriott's hand and gave him a hug. I never thought anything of it. I hug everybody. Well, this was not the Marriott culture. My CEO advised, as he pulled me aside, "You should get to know people before you hug them."

I was mortified. My second day on the job, and I thought my career was ruined. For weeks, I re-lived that scenario repeatedly in my head, thinking what a fool I had made of myself until one day at lunch, I was told that the CEO apologized for me the next time he saw Mr. Marriott after that encounter by explaining that I had just come from the non-profit community. "That Shane is quite a hugger isn't he?" he'd asked Mr. Marriott. Much to his surprise, I'm sure, Mr. Marriott replied, "Yes, and we sure could use a lot more hugging around here."

What a wonderful experience it was learning the "Marriott way." By the time I left, we were a "hugging" foundation.

I then joined the Freddie Mac Foundation as the director. The absolute, greatest outcome of that experience was the expansion of my family.

One Sunday morning, when I was watching "Wednesday's Child, I instantly fell in love with two brothers in need of a family. Moye and Nigel were three and five years old at the time. Moye and Nigel somehow reminded me of KB and me. Not only were they adorable; here was an opportunity to keep two little brothers together. I could not help it; I tried to ignore the feeling, but felt compelled to respond. After speaking to Saint Gloria, I believed our influence could help them grow into healthy, productive young men. Besides, Tiffany was now about to graduate from high school in June; my son David had already graduated and moved into his apartment; and Shane Rico was away at school. The only children in our big house were Brittney and Courtney. Surely, there was room for two more, I rationalized. Whenever I think back, I cannot help but laugh at myself. Who did I think I was…Mr. Josephine Baker?

Tiffany graduated in June, in spite of being quite upset with me for moving from our home in Chantilly, which resulted in her attending a new high school. I totally minimized her predicament because in my educational experience, there had not been school continuity—especially since Tiffany initially said she did not mind, but obliviously felt otherwise. Perhaps if I had stayed anywhere in my life from beginning to end, I would have instinctively known. I really think Tiffany knew how much I wanted us to move, and put aside her own needs. Unfortunately, she reminded everyone who came into her midst all year long of it and struggled in her senior year as a result. It was touch and go there for a while, However, when graduation day came, I knew one overriding factor was all that very mattered: I kept my promise, and I never walked out on her. I was there from birth to graduation. She never knew the kind of rejection and loneliness I had known. In addition, I was so proud that she didn't join the 22 percent teenage pregnancy statistic. Tiffany decided to follow my footsteps when she enlisted in the Navy after graduation. Two months later, Gloria also completed her life goal and finished her master of science degree in information technology from American University. She worked full-time, attended graduate school full-time, and remained on point for a house full of children. Absolutely amazing and brilliant that woman is; I just hope the children get her discipline and brains!

Soon after Gloria's graduation, our two new sons arrived. I was so gung ho about being a new dad that I took a couple of weeks of paternity leave. For me, two weeks off from work was unprecedented. It was an extra-special Christmas with the addition of brothers Moye and Nigel. On that Christmas morning, the twinkle in their eyes said it all.

Looking at my beautiful family reminded me of how much I had overcome in my life and how fortunate I was to have found a way out of the despair I had known most of my life. However, I was becoming increasingly mindful of the greater struggle.

Later in my tenure at the Freddie Mac Foundation, I was extremely pleased to be able to leverage funds from the foundation for children in New York's Administration for Children Services (ACS), and the same foster care system that had been responsible for my care, formerly known as Bureau of Child Welfare. ACS was under the leadership of Nicolas Scopetta and William Bell at the time, and I had the good fortune to develop a good relationship with both of them. Nick and I developed a bond out of our common foster care experience. I was proud that someone who experienced it firsthand was leading the reforms in New York. Because of this friendship, I also developed a relationship with Mayor Giuliani. Because of the city's successful reforms, I was able to convince the foundation to honor the Mayor for his leadership on behalf of New York's foster children. Can you imagine what I felt, given my personal experience in that system, to read headlines like those found in the *New York Post* editorial "Credit Where Credit's Due," And imagine this: "An independent blue-ribbon panel is calling the Giuliani administration's effort to combat child abuse and neglect remarkable. After two years of study, the panel recently released a comprehensive good news report...The results are clear: Real changes are possible at City Agencies. Congratulations to all concerned. Your hard work has paid off." That was reported on December 13, 2000. Then again, February 3, 2005, it was reported that "cases of 2,200 children, or more than 10 percent of all those in foster care, will be transferred to agencies with the best track records in the city's annual performance review. The poorly rated agencies had serious shortcomings in such areas as record keeping, child safety, and monitoring the care of children placed with foster parents." This was inconceivable when I was coming through the system. We would have just been stuck in the poor performing agency. For systemic progress such as this, I encouraged the CEO of Freddie Mac and the CEO of the Foundation to host a grand reception in the Mayor's honor at Battery Park to receive a recognition award. I had the pleasure of presenting the award and introducing the Mayor and I did so with tremendous enthusiasm for obvious reasons. This was personal. My life's work culminated right there in that room. I was able to go back home and recognize the Mayor of my city for leading one of the largest system reform efforts in child welfare. It was personal for me! Heartfelt and very personal: the depth of gratitude to all the talent behind the Mayor instrumental in making that a reality like Nick Scopetta, William Bell, and all the others. During his acceptance speech, the Mayor said to the crowd, "I think Shane Salter should run for Mayor," and the crowd responded with thunderous applause. I relished that moment, but at the same time, I was wary of the fact that my boss at the foundation didn't like her subordinates getting an ounce more of attention than she got, especially when her boss, the CEO of Freddie Mac, was present. I assured the audience that I was flattered, but had no plans to leave Freddie Mac anytime soon. The Mayor invited me back to New York a few weeks later for lunch with him, and we sat and talked in his office for over two and a half hours exchanging our philosophies on leadership and management, talking deeply about his challenges and successes, and mine. I gave him my assurance that what we discussed in that room stayed in that room, and it has. Not one person will ever know. It is amazing to me now. Talking about leadership and management, not knowing September 11 was just a few months away and his life would be transformed yet once more. While having that experience with him, I wanted someone to pinch me. How did I go from being a foster child in New York that nobody wanted and everybody rejected, to sitting there enjoying casual conversation and lunch with the Mayor of New York, If my friends could see me now! Nick whispered afterwards, "Those of us in the cabinet don't even get that much uninterrupted time; he really enjoyed talking with you."

Shortly after that, the White House asked me to join President Bush for the signing of the Safe and Stable Family Act. After attending the signing ceremony with the President, I returned to my office, where my boss informed me that I was terminated effective that day without severance. How painfully ironic, I thought, to be witnessing the signing of the Safe and Stable Families Act that morning, only to have my family totally destabilized that afternoon. I could not believe it. How was I going to take care of my family? With no means of caring for my family other than the honorariums from speaking engagements and those were certainly not consistent enough to live off. Unlike ever before, I was horrified because the stakes had never been so high. My family was depending on me, for security in the way I wanted to depend on mine when I was little. Now I was suddenly without income with two new sons through Wednesday's Child that I was unsure if I could keep. All of this was circling in my head as I tried to also figure out how to go home that evening and keep the news from my family at least that day in order to celebrate grandma's birthday. It was hard. Perhaps the hardest was the unleashing of all my "foster care stuff" as the doorbell rang mid afternoon, I opened it to find my office belongings delivered in cardboard boxes.

Flashbacks of all those times I had been thrown out of homes as a child came racing back. I was so unprepared for it all. However, when there was nowhere else to go, I went where I always go, on my knees. I prayed and God reminded me that everything I have, he gave to me. No one gave me the Freddie Mac Foundation job; he placed me there for that moment in time to learn, to grow, and to contribute. He then went on to let me know that no one can take from you what was not his or hers to give. It was then that I found strength through "No weapon formed against me shall prosper." And I've been singing it ever since. Organizations with missions to strengthen families and children at the very least should never put an employee's family at risk in a manner comparable to the population they seek to serve. However, the Freddie Mac Foundation has made substantial contributions to the welfare of children, youth and families under the leadership of my former CEO during my tenure. One of which I was most proud, was the support we gave during the early stages of the Congressional Coalition on Adoption, Co Chaired By Sen. Mary Landrieu (D) LA and Sen. Larry Craig (R) ID. Under their leadership and with support from many others, The Coalition launched the Congressional Coalition on Adoption Institute. The Congressional Coalition on Adoption Institute (CCAI) is a nonprofit, nonpartisan organization dedicated to raising awareness about the tens of thousands of foster children in this country and the millions of orphans around the world in need of permanent, safe, and loving homes; and to eliminating the barriers that hinder these children from realizing their basic need of a family. The *Angels in Adoption*™ Program is CCAI's signature public awareness program. These "unsung heroes" are selected by members of the US Congress to represents their states at a Washington-based gala given in their honor each September.

CCAI invites all members of Congress to select an individual, family, or organization from their home states who have significantly contributed to changing the lives of children in need; specifically through adoption and foster care. Each Angel and member of Congress is invited to attend the *Angels in Adoption*™ Awards Gala, where they meet and share their personal experiences and involvement in adoption and foster care. In addition, National Angels are selected by the Congressional Directors of CCAI for their work on a national and international scale. If you know of an unsung hero making a difference in the life of a child, consider contacting the congressional representative in their home district to initiate the nomination process for this distinguished award.

The other initiative I was equally proud of was the support we gave to the "Oliver Project" though the Orphan Foundation you know you are doing something right if you can get both Rep. Tom Delay (R) TX and Sen. Hillary Clinton

(D) NY in agreement on an issue. They both supported the organization and attended the dinner that the Orphan Foundation held to highlight the interns.

Although still shell shocked from the Freddie Mac Foundation experience, my next job was Chief of Staff to the Deputy Mayor for Children, Youth, Families, and Elders of the District of Columbia. I consulted with a friend and mentor who at the time had just become the Commissioner of New York's Foster Care System, before accepting the position. Where he said as Chief of Staff, I would learn more in six months, than I would for years in most places. That sealed it for me. What an awesome growth opportunity and professional challenge this was. My mentor was right; every day presented a new learning opportunity. Responding to the complex and competing constituents needs without having my name slandered in the paper as an embarrassment to the Mayor, was one benchmark of success I set for myself. It certainly was not easy, given the agencies for which we had oversight responsibility such as: the Department of Health, Child and Family Services Administration, Department of Human Services, Office of Human Rights, Office of Aging, Department of Parks and Recreation, the State Education Office and Public Library System. With the largest percentage of the city's budget, we had our plates full. It was an incredible experience, quite a rollercoaster ride serving in Mayor Williams' administration. The Mayor was brilliant and under estimated. Just like many of those who journey from foster care. For those reasons and many more, I admired him and felt vested in his success. I couldn't help but look how far in spite of it all, I had come. To be part of an administration filled with incredible talent, and contributing to the renaissance of the Nation's Capital, was beyond my wildest dreams. More rewarding, however, was serving with a Deputy Mayor who was passionate and determined to achieve the gains made on behalf of children in the District of Columbia. As reported by the Council for Court Excellence, the city's compliance with various ASFA deadlines for reaching decisions in child neglect and abuse cases improved steadily, particularly in cases where the child has been removed from home. What perhaps has given me the greatest satisfaction was the city's implementation of the Family Drug Treatment Court., a program that if my mother had the opportunity to access it, I am certain our outcome would have been much more favorable. Modeled after similar programs in New York, Florida, Ohio and Virginia, this program gives mothers the chance to rebuild their lives and their families within the Adoption and Safe Families Act (ASFA) timelines. Substance-abusing mothers whose children are in the DC neglect system receive services through this initiative. Mothers who qualify for the program are permitted to live with their children at the treatment facility while undergoing six months of rigorous, supervised drug treatment. In addition, the women receive job training, and classes in household management, budgeting, and parenting. After six months, the women enter a six-month aftercare program. One of the most significant advantages of the program is that it enables children to stay out of foster care and remain with their mothers. Because the mothers are receiving treatment and no longer using drugs, there is a greater chance that they and their children can become families again. Wow, what a long way we have come, in just my lifetime. Sometimes, it is so hard for me to believe its real when I think about where it all started, what was available then. Yet, I am acutely aware of how great the need remains. We need more treatment facilities like the one just described for families. Could you imagine the impact and overall cost savings if we invested nationwide in programs like that to ensure families remained together. It is the right thing to do and it is less of a burden on taxpayers as well.

After resigning as Chief of Staff, I had no clue what I would do next. In fact, I was somewhat scared, there was no "dream job" I could think of. I had accomplished and experienced all that I could imagine. I knew I needed time to think about what to do next. Then a call came from the Board of Directors at CASA (Court Appointed Special Advocates) of DC, an organization I helped to start before coming to the Mayor's office. Sadly, the first Executive Director hired just had a stroke. I agreed to serve as the Interim Executive Director while I thought through my long-term options. There was no way I could say no. I believed in the mission of the organization and happened to be available. Never did I expect to stay beyond Interim; however, as soon as I started working there, it was like hand in glove. This was my calling. At that moment in time, it was clear I was supposed to return and finish what I had begun. Engaging Washingtonians is part of the solution to support and liberate the 2,800 children that are not living at home in DC's child welfare system.

Wake Up!

I knew that CASA was one of the best-kept secrets or, one could say, best, kept secret solutions to moving children through the child welfare system quickly and safely. This grassroots DC organization needed strong visionary leadership that would garner the support necessary to sustain the mission for as many years the need exist for neglected or abused children. Since I strongly believe in community engagement and activism, this was a challenge I was prepared to accept. The one caveat was figuring out if I could live off a non-profit salary with a family. I struggled over it, and we ultimately found a way to work a salary out so that the compromise would not have a substantial impact. It was liberating to not make money the issue. My decision was about a calling that I had to be obedient to; everything in my life prepared me for this opportunity to lead. I was truly stepping out on faith. I have never regretted my decision. The staff, volunteers and Board at CASA for Children of DC has made tremendous strides while advocating on behalf of the children. I am always pursuing funding from every viable source so that the citizens of the Washington Metropolitan Area will have the opportunity to volunteer as an advocate give voice and hope to a child.

CASA for Children of the District of Columbia recruits, trains and supervises community volunteers to serve as court appointed special advocates according to national standards. These advocates investigate, monitor and recommend to judges timely action that is in the best interests of the child victims.

The goal of CASA is to see that each child is placed as quickly as possible in a permanent home that is safe, nurturing and free from violence. In a system where dockets overflow and professional caseloads make individual attention challenging, volunteers ensure that the needs of each child are met. By providing objective, detailed information and recommendations to the courts, volunteers help to expedite these children through the child welfare system and into adoptive families.

Family Court judges agree that CASA for Children of the District of Columbia advocates are an essential component when important decisions are made regarding the future of child abuse victims and their families. Volunteers, dedicated staff and a committed Board of Directors work together as part of this nonprofit youth advocacy agency. CASA volunteers are an ethnically and culturally diverse group. Each one participates in 30 hours of training with experts in the field, and each volunteer is evaluated carefully before being assigned a case.

At CASA for Children of DC, the emphasis is placed on collaboration for the sake of children. We know that courtroom advocacy alone, even with hundreds of committed volunteers; will not ensure that each of our children will be able to return home or to find a new adoptive family. Only through widespread community support and collaboration can we possibly hope to meet the multiple needs of our children, especially for kinship, foster and adoptive homes.

At CASA for Children of DC, we work hard to prevent children from traveling this journey. However, it takes all of us. Without your help, the work cannot be done. Please consider making a generous tax-deductible contribution to:

> CASA for Children of DC 919 Eighteenth Street, NW
> Suite #510
> Washington, DC 20006 Or www.casadc.org
> Att: ***Trouble Don't Last Always***

Wake Up!—The Child Abuse Court Advocacy Movement

There are currently over 900 CASA programs around the country. This is an opportunity for everyone to get involved and make a difference. One way to ensure that the system is held accountable and that the "Shanes" out there have the greatest chance to hold on to their childhoods and grow within a healthy family where they are loved and nurtured is to become a CASA. Get on board and become a part of this movement led by the people for the people. We need more CASAs of color from the communities where the greatest numbers of children enter foster care. We need ordinary citizens willing to step up, speak out, and say, I will get to know this child, I will make sure he or she is never forgotten about, I will hold my government and myself responsible for ensuring that children of abuse and neglect have a chance to have their full potential nurtured as they transition to adulthood. I will go into court and help judges make the best possible decision about where that child should live, what school he or she should go to, what educational resources he or she needs, as if they were my own. I will *Wake Up* the system and be his voice in court. You can do that much, after just 30 hours of training. If this message speaks to your heart, then consider yourself "awake." Now that you have "*Woken Up,*" *do not just sit there. Put this book down and call 1800 628-3223 or visit www.nationalcasa. org*

The national movement to have the independent voice of child victims heard in court began in the 1960s. Judges realized they were making far-reaching decisions about the lives of children without hearing the unique perspective of the child. Some judges asked social workers or friends to informally investigate child abuse cases and make recommendations about what would best serve the needs and interests of the child. The first volunteer guardian ad litem (GAL) program serving abused and neglected children was organized by King County Judge David Soukup in 1977 in Seattle, Washington. In the following years, word of the success of the King County program spread like wildfire, and similar programs began all over the United States. Because some state statutes require the guardian ad litem to be an attorney, the term Court Appointed Special Advocate—CASA—was coined to describe volunteers from the local community trained to serve as advocates for abused and neglected children involved in juvenile court proceedings. In 1982, the National CASA Association, Inc. was established to serve as an umbrella organization for the growing number of programs in the country. National CASA provides information, technical assistance, research, and training. National CASA also sponsors an annual national conference and has a grants program that annually awards millions of dollars to state and local CASA and guardian ad litem programs. Membership in National CASA is open to both individuals and programs.

ADVANTAGES OF THE NATIONAL CASA ASSOCIATION

Efficiency

• Because CASA is a program of citizen volunteers, funds invested deliver a quick and impressive return in terms of children served. Federal funding is turned around within months as competitive, peer-reviewed grants to CASA programs. A grant of $40,000 can support hiring one volunteer supervisor, which can result in an additional 60–80 children served within the first year.

• By contracting with the National CASA Association to oversee the CASA grants program, the Department of Justice is able to assure effective utilization of funds, in compliance with *federal regulations* and *National CASA standards*.

• Federal funding allows a large number of communities (est. 250 in 2004) to expand volunteer advocacy without becoming dependent upon this single source of revenue. CASA programs are supported by a mix of private, local and state government funding, in addition to the federal grant project.

• Funds administered by National CASA can be effectively leveraged at the local level. As an example, National CASA targeted grants to build the capacities of urban programs in one of those years. These programs raised $2.4 million in additional funding, increasing volunteers by 51% and service to children by 65%.

Cost Effectiveness

• The child welfare system could not afford to provide a comparable level of advocacy through non-volunteer approaches. CASA volunteers have contributed 10 million hours of advocacy for children in one year. If compensated to perform such a role, the total would be more than $496 million.

• By helping to reduce time spent unnecessarily in foster care, CASA can reduce child welfare costs. In 2001, an estimated 540,000 children were in foster care, at an estimated cost to Americans of $16 billion. If the median length of stay in foster care (19 months) were shortened for CASA children by just *one month,* it would realize a savings of approximately $1.3 billion.

Better Service to Children

• Low CASA caseloads mean the courts can make better decisions for children. CASA volunteers handle just 1 or 2 cases at a time, so that they can give each child's case the *sustained, personal* attention he or she deserves.

• Complex cases receive more attention so they can move forward in a timely way. CASA volunteers are typically appointed to the more complex children's cases—those where there are multiple risk factors which must be fully understood in order to make a placement decision that will be in the child's best interests.

Please Consider Making Tax-Deductible Contributions Directly

The National CASA phone number is 800-628-3233 and their websites is www.nationalcasa.org and www.casanet.org.

> **National CASA Association**
> **100 W. Harrison, N. Tower**
> **Suite #500**
> **Seattle, WA 98119**
> **Att: *Trouble Don't Last Always***

Wake Up!—USKIDS Are Waiting

There are close to 600,000 children still languishing in the foster care system. Children throughout the United States are waiting for permanent families. They are school-aged, teenagers, or may be brothers and sisters needing a home together. Some have special physical, emotional or educational needs. More than 60 percent come from minority cultures. You will find over 3000 of these waiting children on the AdoptUSKids website. ACT NOW! No child or sibling group in America should have his or her childhood snatched away and feel that nobody cares. We can do so much better. Please visit. www.adoptuskids.org to consider becoming a foster or adoptive parent.

EPILOGUE

I've seen countless decisions made at the convenience of those who look nothing like the children represented in the system, but have wealth, influence and no regard for the real bottom line…"the children." I have heard all too often many use "the best interest" of children interwoven in sentences because it is the proper thing to say. However, it is their *individual* interest, or "the agency's interest" that is clearly paramount. This is particularly evident when I look at how young people who have grown up in foster care are treated. After years and years of guardianship from agency and government leaders who've had access to a full complement of support services, from private schools to clinical providers, the ugly reality is that these services are not leveraged or coordinated properly, and an overwhelming majority of youth are grossly unprepared when they leave. There are no outcome standards by which the public can hold those being trusted with the healthy growth and development of victimized children accountable. Would you keep sending your cars to the same mechanic if each car came back with a broken engine after you originally sent it in for a brake job? Then why when it is children, do we keep sending them to grow-up in public and private agencies when it is widely known that when they arrive from their families as victims of abuse or neglect, after months or years of government intervention, many leave having been more neglected and abused and without skills, resources or support to lead a successful adult life. Why not just leave them with their families and take half of the same money used in government services to assist with breaking the intergenerational cycles of neglect and substance and physical abuse. It is critical that those who work with youth at risk absolutely believe they can achieve unforeseeable heights. I am not talking about the kind of belief that sounds good in a room full of folks when it's the popular thing to believe. I mean, believe as if it were what you dreamed and aspired for your own child before he or she were even conceived. Our youth are surrounded by caregivers who act and think that the present circumstances always predict future outcomes. If you haven't figured it out by now, I sure did. One of the reasons I'm sure I was meant to endure and survive, was to come back and let you know that just isn't so. However, when you look at our youth in all of their pain and broken heartedness, and all you can do is pity, bow your head, mumble under your breath and say, "Um Um Um…I know where he'll end up."…Then maybe because of you, that's exactly where he will end up. I once interviewed for a position at a renowned medical institution in Baltimore, Maryland that provides therapeutic foster care and a host of other comprehensive services for special needs children. After completing my interviews with a licensed clinical social worker, and a psychiatrist along with three other members of the executive management team, I withdrew from consideration as a finalist. I found after learning that I was once a foster child, they were all asking the same question with different variations on the theme: "How did you make it?" Well there is nothing wrong with that question on face value. However, it became clear that they really didn't believe that my professional accomplishments were within my grasp. Certainly, the prevailing question was how did you get there, to merit an audience with each of them as a candidate to work in that reputable institution among such a distinguished group of professionals? Look, I believe it comes down to this, I needed then like our youth need today, the support of a caring committed adult network that believed in my possibilities. I needed then like our youth need today, to be held accountable for confronting my fears of attachment as early as possible with the support of committed consistent well-qualified professionals. It is then they will as young adults begin working to engage comfortably in social relationships instead of sabotaging and running from them. Caregivers must make working through the issues resulting from the trauma endured through abandonment and false love higher on the priority scale.

When it comes to our youth, it's just this simple or as the old folks use to say, let me make it plain:

> If you think they *won't* make it, they'll feel your vibe and probably won't. If you believe they *can* make it, they will absorb it and probably will.
>
> If you *teach* and show him to make it, then you've done your job with excellence.

Mine has been an incredible journey, through trouble and triumph. The true blessing is although scorned and covered with scars, I am still strong determined and full of courage. All of my life, I've been up against all kinds of odds. I became driven and determined to make it to the finish line when confronted with the reality of the multigenerational devastation that drugs, neglect and abuse has had on my family. While I feel we've made progress, I'm not sure if I'll break the cycle at times. Sometimes I feel like I'm repeating it. It's a constant struggle within. This journey I traveled has led me down several paths: as a child in search of the love and the security family brings, a teen parent, a single parent, an adoptive parent. Then as an executive of one of the larger foster care agencies in Washington, DC, a philanthropist within a corporate foundation, a civil servant, and now as CEO of an organization energized with advocates for abused and neglected children. Having experienced all these perspectives gives me a unique outlook on many of the issues facing children and families in our country. Although much has been accomplished over the years through emerging advocates, there is still a long way to go in order to fully maximize the full potential of all of America's children. Unfortunately, after children are placed in foster care, they can expect to be moved from home to home. This is why it is so important for the family and the community the children are from to act quickly as a resource for children before further harm occurs. That is how we make a wrong right. If that child has a culturally competent CASA (Court Appointed Special Advocate), then that process can be expedited by ensuring unlike in my case where I did not have a CASA that the child does not get lost in the cracks. Perhaps a culturally competent CASA from the South Bronx or surrounding area would have ensured my mother got the treatment she needed and if she did not comply, expedited the process of terminating her parental rights. Granted things were different then, but another set of eyes, pressuring the numerous players in the system, and keeping the judge motivated through court reports with recommendations, might have made a difference and helped to keep my brother and me together. That is why I wrote this book, because the solution is within our grasp. Trouble does not *have* to last always. All it takes is for you, our neighbor and me to declare it and make it so. Just imagine that one neighbor who chooses not to become an adoptive parent decides instead to foster parent a child. The other neighbor, who is not able to foster parent a child, perhaps is well suited to be a CASA. We all have a role in the healing of an abused child just commit to finding yours and the rewards will be more than you can imagine.

Research indicates that 33 percent of homeless people and 80 percent of our prison population were once in foster care. The numbers are equally alarming when it comes to those in mental health institutions. However, this does not have to be so if our children have the support of a caring adult in their life. As for me, ultimately, the struggles I have endured over the years left a few bruises and scars that I must continue to work through.

My greatest challenges have been with social and interpersonal relationships. I have struggled in this area all of my life. Consequently, I find myself isolated and lonely most of the time. I often hear from people that "I'm just too much to handle." That means many things to different people. Another casualty has been my own family. Although we still function as a family, I have not lived with Gloria and the children for last few years. I have chosen for the first time in my life to live alone and face my demons. I am working overtime through my stuff to be the best man I can be. I am only now just beginning to learn who I really am and how to love me. In order to do that, I had to stop acting like a grown foster child showing up with a new mask, in a new home, hoping that the people will like me enough not to reject me. After all these years, right before my grandmother died, I started pulling the mask off little by little with the hopes of finding Shane somewhere underneath it. Grandma and Gloria gave me the strength to start my journey of healing, with their love and support; I discovered I had nothing else to give to anyone until I figured some basic things out...It took almost a lifetime for me to understand that when you are grounded in a comprehensive understanding of yourself, truth, and love of God, then your foundation is rock solid and what grows from there can't be shaken. Those are now my core values.

The capacity to listen to others has always been a challenge for me in relationships. I find myself interrupting before the other person has completed their thought. For a long time I wasn't aware of how often I did this, how annoying it is, or how I was perceived by others as a result. I just knew that people seemed to shut down after a while when talking with me. Some of this was simply fear of intimacy, my fears of being still, close and silent with anyone. I've always been afraid of silence. I remember silence. It was very silent when my mother left, and I never wanted to hear it again.

However, the other fact of the matter is I never knew how easily distracted I get during conversations, I guess because it was this way all of my life. This was simply normal to me, yet it was having a devastating impact on relationships. I have always been extremely intense. I never knew how much intense behavior and style affected others. It was through adult work that I began to realize that intense people could come across as arrogant and rude.

Others often misunderstand me as self-absorbed. For most of my life I just thought, along with everything else, I was just screwed up, from the times as a little boy sitting in trashcans in first grade, having my mouth washed out with soap in third grade, all kinds of trouble and punishments, difficulty socializing with people. I remember those days as a 7-year-old kid, sitting with Dad Jamison and watching "60 Minutes," instead of playing with other kids and toys and how great that felt then. Not that there is anything wrong with a little kid watching "60 Minutes," I was just always intense and serious. After my grandmother died...realizing how disconnected I'd been feeling most of my life, I just couldn't stand it anymore I sought help from everywhere in order to better engage and relate to people. As I have recently discovered, the one common thread all throughout my life was my attention deficit disorder (ADD). What I never knew was how much more to that condition there is than what most of us hear about in sound bites. It is more than just the image we have of the hot-wired kid bouncing off the walls. Many people with ADD remain feeling like outsiders, not knowing how to connect. After years of disconnecting, well, most outsiders just stop trying to be a part of the world around them. Many of us struggle with addictions as a means of self-medicating; I have struggled with mine and refused to be overcome by them given my family history. There is a heavy price I pay by making the choice to lead my complex life as an open book. I have accepted that price given the outcome and effect I have seen it has had on the lives of others, particularly youth.

As I sign off, there have been many changes in legislation since I've entered foster care that give me reason to be hopeful, some of which I've influenced directly and others perhaps indirectly. One firsthand experience was when I had the opportunity to testify on behalf of the Multi-ethnic Placement Act (MEPA), along with Rev. Tally of One Church One Child, Rev. Jesse Jackson of the Rainbow Coalition, and Joe Kroll, of North American Council on Adoptable Children. The overriding goals of MEPA (amended in 1996 to assess interethnic adoptions provisions) were to reduce the length of time children spend in out-of home care, and to prevent discrimination in placement decisions. Also in 1996, the Personal Responsibility and Work Opportunity Reconciliation Act replaced AFDC with Temporary Assistance to Needy families (TANF). The goals of TANF are to assist low-income families with children so the children can be cared for in their own homes, reduce dependency by promoting job preparation, reduce out-of-wedlock pregnancies and encourage the formation and maintenance of two-parent families.

Then came the Adoption and Safe Families Act of 1997 (ASFA), which represented the most significant change in federal child welfare law since the Adoption Assistance and Child Welfare Act of 1980. In general, ASFA is intended to promote primacy of child safety and timely decisions while clarifying "reasonable efforts" and continuing family preservation. When I started sharing my experience in 1989 of growing up and aging out of foster care with no family, it was a law such as this I only dreamed of but never thought would happen. Had ASFA been in place, requiring my mother to get the help she needed and the state to have a permanent plan for me and my brother within twelve months, maybe I would have been able to hold on to some of my childhood. Perhaps, instead of acting as my brother's parent, and enduring ongoing abuse, neglect and rejection,

I might have thrived in a loving family. I am glad there is a clock that starts ticking for all the adults involved from the time a child is traumatically removed from home. The clock includes accountability for the professionals responsible for family supports and strengthening as well as accountability for the parents who are unable to care for their child at the time. One day in a child's life is equivalent to a year in that of an adult. All of us within the communities our children come from and those responsible for their oversight when removed must commit to the preservation of children's childhoods. Fortunately, my two youngest sons benefited from ASFA and became available for adoption at an early enough age, where the interventions provided by Gloria and me have the greatest chance at succeeding. How they arrived to us, in contrast to how they have developed over the few years we have had them, is a testimony unto itself. Their potential is being nurtured and their sibling bond has been preserved. This is what lets me know that all of the sacrifices made by my family have been worth it. To see that it hasn't just all fallen on deaf ears, but that changes are being made, reform is occurring, people are beginning to acknowledge the treatment of foster children in this nation is unacceptable, lets me know that my mother's living, my grandmother's living and my great grand-father's living was not in vain. Ralph Waldo Emerson writes:

> *To laugh often and much; To win the respect of intelligent people and affection of children; To earn the appreciation of honest critics and endure the betrayal of false friends; to appreciate beauty, to find the best in others; to leave the world a bit better, whether by a healthy child, a garden patch or a redeemed social condition; to know even one life has breathed easier because you have lived. This is to have succeeded.*

If this is true, then great-granddad was right that day he uttered those words that sent chills down my spine as he gave me my baby shoe. This has been a life with pain and purpose, a life like all others with difficulties failures and successes; a life that before formed in the womb; was ordained by God, I hope he is pleased.

978-0-595-34796-4
0-595-34796-7

Printed in the United States
37837LVS00005B/176

9 780595 347964